W9-AXP-891

THE BEST OF
BROCHURE DESIGN 6

ROCKPORT

THE BEST OF
BROCHURE DESIGN 6

GLOUCESTER MASSACHUSETTS

ROCKPORT PUBLISHERS

© 2001 by Rockport Publishers, Inc.
First published in paperback in 2003

All rights reserved. No part of this book may be
reproduced in any form without written permission
of the copyright owners. All images in this
book have been reproduced with the knowledge
and prior consent of the artists concerned and
no responsibility is accepted by producer, publisher,
or printer for any infringement of copyright
or otherwise, arising from the contents of this
publication. Every effort has been made to ensure
that credits accurately comply with
information supplied.

First published in the United States of America by
Rockport Publishers, Inc.
33 Commercial Street
Gloucester, Massachusetts 01930-5089
Telephone: (978) 282-9590
Fax: (978) 283-2742
www.rockpub.com

ISBN 1-56496-969-X

10 9 8 7 6 5 4 3 2 1

Design: Stoltze Design

Printed in China

1 > **CORPORATE BROCHURES + ANNUAL REPORTS**   008

2 > **PRODUCT BROCHURES**   050

3 > **SERVICE BROCHURES**   090

4 > **NONPROFIT, EDUCATIONAL, INSTITUTIONAL + HEALTHCARE BROCHURES**   136

5 > **SELF-PROMOTIONAL BROCHURES**   158

6 > **ARTS, ENTERTAINMENT + EVENT BROCHURES**   182

▸ **DIRECTORY OF DESIGN FIRMS**   202

▸ **INDEX**   206

TECNICI CON UNA FORTE IDENTITÀ, FUNZIONALI, CREATIVI, UNICI E RARI PER MIGLIORARE LA QUALITÀ DELLA VITA. IDEE DI PRODOTTO, MA ANCHE DI ORGANIZZAZIONE E DI SERVIZI PER RISPONDERE SEMPRE MEGLIO ALLE DOMANDE DEL NUOVO MILLENNIO

ARE BORN FROM INTUITION, FROM THE RESEARCH AND EXPERIENCE GAINED FROM TECHNOLOGY. TOGETHER WITH CLIENTS, TRENDS AND MARKET DEMANDS. AIM: TO CREATE TECHNO FABRICS WITH A STRONG IDENTITY, FUNCTIONAL, CREATIVE AND UNIQUE TO IMPROVE THE QUALITY OF LIFE. PRODUCT IDEAS BUT ALSO ORGANIZATION AND SERVICES TO RESPOND INCREASINGLY

CORPORATE BROCHURES +
ANNUAL REPORTS

DESIGN FIRM › Gregory Thomas Associates
ART DIRECTORS › Gregory Thomas, Alice Flanjak, David La Cava
DESIGNERS › Gregory Thomas, Alice Flanjak, David La Cava
ILLUSTRATOR/PHOTOGRAPHER › In House
COPYWRITERS › David La Cava, Todd Hays
CLIENT › Baskin-Robbins International
TOOLS (SOFTWARE/PLATFORM) › Cut and paste montage; no computer
PRINTING PROCESS › Offset

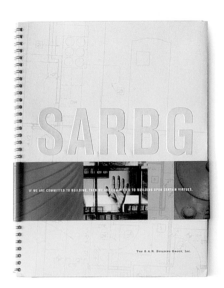

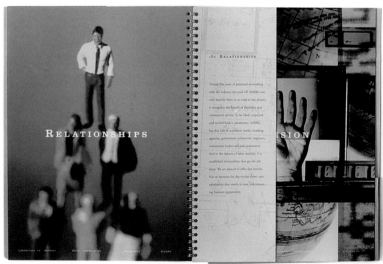

DESIGN FIRM > Base Art Co.
ART DIRECTOR > Terry Alan Rohrbach
DESIGNER > Terry Alan Rohrbach
ILLUSTRATOR/PHOTOGRAPHER > Photonica
COPYWRITER > Hilary Rubin
CLIENT > The SAR Building Group
TOOLS (SOFTWARE/PLATFORM) > QuarkXPress, Photoshop, Macintosh G4
PAPER STOCK > Strobe 100 lb. text; Kaos 100 lb. cover
PRINTING PROCESS > Offset, with foil-stamped emboss

TUTTLINGEN FÜR
Kulturfreunde

Tuttlingen für Kulturfreunde

Für Kulturfreunde ist in Tuttlingen das ganze Jahr über etwas geboten. Musik, Theater und Kabarettabende, aber auch Sportevents wie die DTB-Gala, die große Sportgala des Deutschen Turnerbundes, finden Sie in fast jeder Woche des Jahres.

Beim Honberg Sommer, dem großen Zeltfestival auf dem Honberg, treten jeweils über zwei Wochen im Juli Weltstars, aktuelle deutsche Künstler und regionale Acts auf. Freunde von Rock, Pop, Folk, Jazz, Soul und anderen musikalischen Stilrichtungen kommen hier auf ihre Kosten.

Oder darf es ein Comedy-, Varieté- oder Kabarettsahnestückchen sein? In der Reihe „Bühne im Anger" im Stadtteil Möhringen präsentiert die Stadt ausgesuchte Kleinkunstveranstaltungen aus den Sparten Kabarett, Chanson, Comedy, Varieté und Musik. Der enge Kontakt zu den auftretenden Künstlern und die tolle Atmosphäre in der Angerhalle machen jede Veranstaltung zu einem unvergesslichen Erlebnis.

Das Honbergfestival mit internationalen Musikern

Tuttlingen für Gesellige

In Tuttlingen wird das ganze Jahr über viel gefeiert und gefestet.
Im Februar hat die schwäbisch-alemannische Fasnet Tuttlingen fest im Griff. Spätestens am dem „Schmotzig Dunschtig" übernehmen die Narren in der Stadt das Regiment und da gibt es dann vor allem im Stadtteil Möhringen einige Ereignisse, die Sie nicht versäumen sollten.

Das „Fest der freundschaftlichen Begegnung" findet alljährlich im Juni/Juni auf dem Marktplatz statt. Hier vereinten Menschen aus über 70 Ländern Eindrücke von ihren kulturellen Besonderheiten und gastronomischen Spezialitäten.

Am letzten Juniwochenende hat das Tuttlinger Stadtfest seinen festen Platz. An über 100 Ständen werden Unterhaltung, Information, Speisen und Getränke angeboten. Eine Gastronomiestraße, Straßenkünstler, der Stadtfestmarkt in der Bahnholzstraße und ein buntes Programm auf zahlreichen Bühnen sorgen für eine großartige Atmosphäre auf beiden Seiten der Donau.

Stadtfest im Juni

Mittelalterlicher Markt

Weinstraße im August

Im August können Sie auf der „Tuttlinger Weinstraße" den Urlaub in vollen Zügen genießen. Rund um den Place de Draguignan bieten Ihnen Tuttlinger Wirte ein abwechslungsreiches gastronomisches Angebot. Bei einem attraktiven musikalischen Rahmenprogramm darf es dann auch mal das eine oder andere Viertele mehr sein.

TUTTLINGEN FÜR
Gesellige

7

DESIGN FIRM › revoLUZion - Studio für Design
ART DIRECTOR › Bernd Luz
DESIGNERS › Bernd Luz, Timo Wenda
ILLUSTRATOR/PHOTOGRAPHER › Bernd Luz
COPYWRITER › Sonja Liebsch
CLIENT › Stadt Tuttlingen
TOOLS (SOFTWARE/PLATFORM) › QuarkXPress, Macintosh

DESIGN FIRM > Emery Vincent Design
ART DIRECTOR > Garry Emery
DESIGNER > Emery Vincent Design
CLIENT > Bligh Voller Nield Architects
TOOLS (SOFTWARE/PLATFORM) > QuarkXPress, Illustrator, Photoshop

**AFTERMARKET
TECHNOLOGY CORP.**

DESIGN FIRM > Critt Graham + Associates
ART DIRECTOR > Deborah Pinals
DESIGNER > Kimie Ishii
ILLUSTRATOR > Kimie Ishii
PHOTOGRAPHER > Michael Grecco
COPYWRITER > Mary Ryan
CLIENT > Aftermarket Technology Corp.
TOOLS (SOFTWARE/PLATFORM) > Macintosh
PAPER STOCK > Fox River Coronado, text; Champion Carnival, cover
PRINTING PROCESS > Offset

DEAR FELLOW STOCKHOLDERS:

It is my privilege to present ATC's 1999 Annual Report. Clearly, 1999 was a year of unprecedented change for our Company. When I joined ATC in late December 1998, the Company had lost sight of its most important constituency – its customers. My priorities in coming on board were clear. Establish ATC as a customer-focused and performance-driven organization. Restore ATC to consistent growth and profitability. Restore our stockholders' faith in the long-term future of ATC.

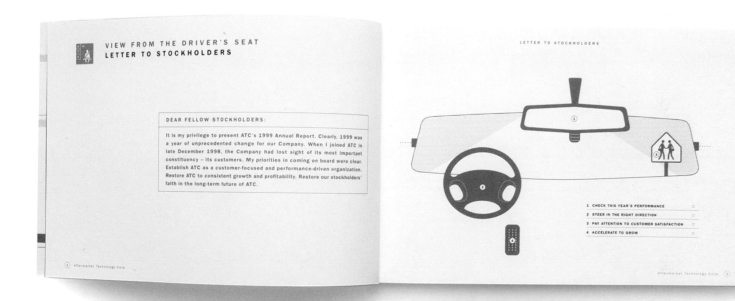

1   CHECK THIS YEAR'S PERFORMANCE
2   STEER IN THE RIGHT DIRECTION
3   PAY ATTENTION TO CUSTOMER SATISFACTION
4   ACCELERATE TO GROW

BE**UNSTOPPABLE**

Compaq is the *NonStop* Internet Company.

That's a pretty bold thing to say, for sure. But it describes, in fact, both how we're working and what we're delivering every day all around the world to help individuals and corporations compete and win in this new networked world.

The details get technical very quickly. But the essence and excitement are easy to explain. We're assembling or assembling all the elements involved - from platforms to services - for NonStop business performance and anywhere, anytime access to the network. We're helping our customers become, quite literally, unstoppable.

How can we say?

But any company can describe itself any way it wants to. We'd like to show you how we're doing it. Right now.

UN
STOP
PABLE

DESIGN FIRM > Critt Graham + Associates
ART DIRECTOR > Kai Siang Toh
DESIGNER > Kai Siang Toh
PHOTOGRAPHER > George Lange
COPYWRITER > Chuck Boyer
CLIENT > Compaq Computer Corporation
TOOLS (SOFTWARE/PLATFORM) > Macintosh
PAPER STOCK > Appleton Utopia
PRINTING PROCESS > Offset

how do you handle 100 customer queries an hour, then 1,000,000 an hour?

how do you deploy applications on the Internet quickly?

how do you hook up everything so that it works

how do you win in the Internet economy   with everything else ... all the time?

how do you run e-commerce and e-business NonStop™?

how do you gain access to the Internet from anywhere, anytime?

and how do you find the coolest stuff to make it all work for you?

24 × 7 × Compaq

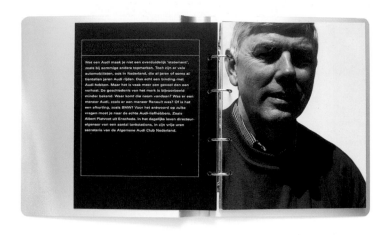

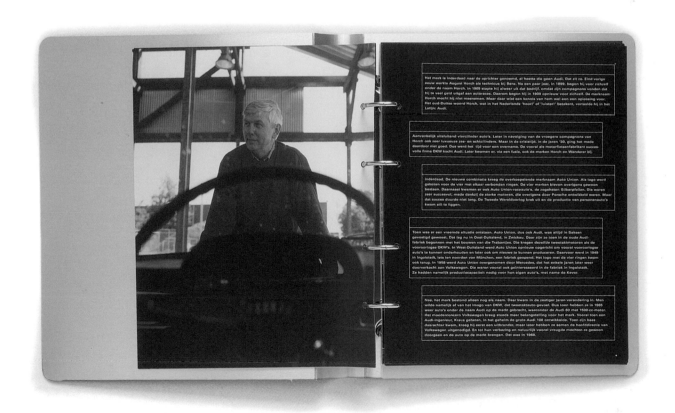

DESIGN FIRM › LA Weekly
ART DIRECTOR › Bill Smith
DESIGNER › Bill Smith
CLIENT › LA Weekly
TOOLS (SOFTWARE/PLATFORM) › QuarkXPress, Photoshop

LA WEEKLY

Simultaneously we sought to provide real alternative thinking and options, whether it was through covering holistic health, visionary human-potential-movement leaders, or solutions to social conditions proffered by local grassroots activists.

On the cultural front, first off we wanted to be a real writer's paper. Also, we had a vision of creating a home base for the unheard smart voices, the new visions, and the artistic creativity exploding in the community — for instance, we opened the pages to the power of the punk and new wave music movements and put together a remarkable team of movie reviewers.

A big part of the vision was to help forge a real citywide community out of what we found to be a collection of adjacent neighborhoods that scarcely knew about each other. We sought to show readers the richness of who they were, the wealth of remarkable places and people all around the L.A. basin, and the creative and intellectual juices actually surging here outside the entertainment industry. Our vision was extremely democratic — we wanted to be the people's hip paper that celebrated the rebel in everyone. We very much wanted to be a paper that people took personally because it had heart and soul as well as good information.

— Jay Levin, Founding Editor

20 YEARS OF LA WEEKLY

It's hard to imagine life in Los Angeles without the *LA Weekly.* Since the first edition appeared 20 years and over 1,000 issues ago, there have been millions of words, photos, ads, cartoons and illustrations; thousands of bands, movies, plays and books reviewed; popular and unpopular positions taken, readers moved and offended, lives and a city transformed. For a whole generation, it's always been there, letting people know what's happening, helping to define L.A., telling stories, offering opinions. And, like that first issue, it's still free.

2

3

magazine called *L.A. Style,* edited by Joie Davidow. The magazine, the result of the fashion boom of the mid-'80s, catered to advertisers and readers who were already familiar with the *Weekly's* format but wanted a glossy vehicle. During the mid-'80s, *L.A. Style* was one of the fastest-growing magazines in the country and winner of many design awards. In 1988, *L.A. Style* was sold to American Express Publishing.

Throughout the 1980s, *LA Weekly* continued to cover the city — and the nation and the world — from an alternative point of view. Its groundbreaking coverage of the conflicts in Central America, environmental issues and the local arts scene generated widespread publicity, won numerous awards and played a significant role in shaping the life of the city. In-depth articles on politics, on poverty and race, on culture, which could not be found in any other publication, caused elected officials to respond and citizens to become active.

In 1988, as Jay Levin became involved in other

LA Weekly's groundbreaking coverage of the conflicts in Central America, environmental issues and the local arts scene generated widespread publicity, won numerous awards and played a significant role in shaping the life of the city.

THE LIST OF L.A.'S FIVE MOST UNDERREPORTED STORIES OF '86 INCLUDED THE PERILS OF OVERDEVELOPMENT, THE AEROSPACE INDUSTRY'S WAR ON A PEACE ORGANIZATION, AND THE COUNTY'S AMBIVALENCE TOWARD THE NEEDY.

10

11

The *Weekly* would cover the offbeat in L.A., not by those pointing a touristic finger and saying, "Oh, isn't this odd?" but by those who lived it.

CONTINUING IN ITS COVERAGE OF THE BURGEONING HOLISTIC HEALTH MOVEMENT, THE *WEEKLY* PROFILED FOUR L.A. HEALERS WITH DISTINCTLY DIFFERENT METHODS.

ON THE EVE OF THE CALIFORNIA NUCLEAR FREEZE INITIATIVE CAMPAIGN, THE *WEEKLY* PROFILED A LEADER OF THE ANTI-NUCLEAR WAR MOVEMENT AND A SURVIVOR OF HIROSHIMA.

Jay Levin, a journalist who was editor of Flynt Publications' L.A. *Free Press* when it folded in 1978, had a vision of Los Angeles as a disparate group of towns that could be linked together and galvanized by a newspaper like the *Weekly* — one that would inform readers all over the city about what was going on in the arts, politics, movies and music. The *Weekly* would cover the offbeat in L.A., not by those pointing a touristic finger and saying, "Oh, isn't this odd?" but by those who lived it. It would create a sense of community among the myriad local neighborhoods.

After the demise of the *Free Press,* Levin approached local businesses and entertainment figures for their support of a new weekly paper in L.A. Actor-producer Michael Douglas and entrepreneur Pete Kameron were among the original investors in the project and remained on its board of directors for many years.

In November of 1978, with Jay Levin as editor, Joie Davidow as Calendar editor

4

5

CORPORATE CITIZENSHIP for The 21st Century

CORPORATE CITIZENSHIP
For The 21st Century

APPLIED MATERIALS®

DESIGN FIRM › Melissa Passehl Design
ART DIRECTOR › Melissa Passehl
DESIGNER › Melissa Passehl
PHOTOGRAPHER › Robert Cardin
COPYWRITER › Susan Sharpe
CLIENT › Applied Materials
TOOLS (SOFTWARE/PLATFORM) › Macintosh, QuarkXPress
PAPER STOCK › Starwhite Vicksburg
PRINTING PROCESS › Four-color PMS

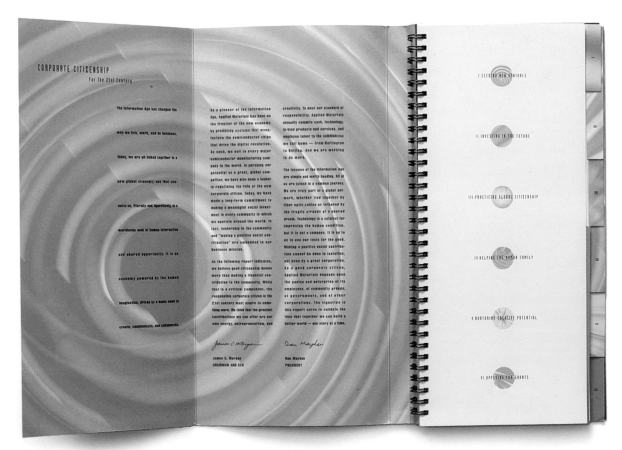

DESIGN FIRM > Country Companies Design Services
ART DIRECTOR > Tracy Griffin Sleeter
DESIGNER > Tracy Griffin Sleeter
PHOTOGRAPHER > Stock Photography
COPYWRITER > Greg Martin
CLIENT > Agency
TOOLS (SOFTWARE/PLATFORM) > Macintosh
PAPER STOCK > Frasier
PRINTING PROCESS > Offset by original Smith printing

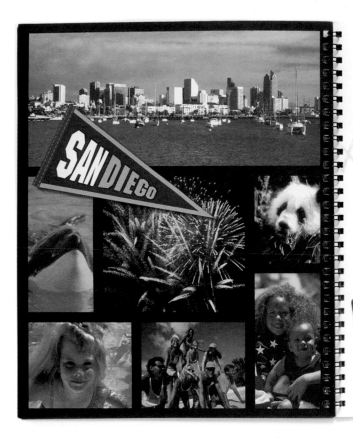

SAN DIEGO
THE BIG DANCE
JUNE 30 - JULY 5, 2001

THE BIG DANCE
HYATT REGENCY SAN DIEGO
SAN DIEGO, CALIFORNIA
JUNE 30 - JULY 5, 2001

What better way to reward your efforts than a trip the entire family will enjoy - to beautiful San Diego, California? If you've never been there, or haven't been there for awhile, you'll be amazed how much there is to do and see.

San Diego is an excellent place the whole family can enjoy. If you're looking for a wild time, you'll find three of the wildest just minutes away - Sea World, Wild Animal Park and the world-famous San Diego Zoo. Looking to enjoy the weather? Rent some bikes, skates or kayaks and soak up the sunshine on Mission Bay or along any of the city's 70 miles of beach.

If golf is your game, you'll like what San Diego County has to offer - 50 public courses to challenge all levels of golfer. From desert landscapes to country hillsides to views of the Pacific, San Diego has it all, including Torrey Pines Golf Course - home of the Buick Invitational.

Want something a little more relaxing? Enjoy lunch at one of San Diego's ocean-view restaurants. Go antique shopping, stroll the boutiques or take a quiet walk along the beach at sunset. Finish off the day in Gaslamp Quarter, where you'll find one of the city's liveliest nighttime street scenes.

Of course, what would July 4th be without a picnic and fireworks? Following a picnic with all our Big Dance qualifiers and their families, enjoy a front row seat to fireworks right from the grounds of your hotel - the Hyatt Regency San Diego, located on San Diego Bay.

Fun for everyone – that's what San Diego has to offer. And it's a fitting reward for making it to The Big Dance.

Here's how you do it:

QUALIFICATION CRITERIA
Contest Period:
December 1, 1999 - November 30, 2000

Requirements
Agents: Must be ranked in Top 640, based on Contest Credits
Must have produced at least 48 Contest Units

Agencies: Must be ranked in Top 64, based on Contest Credits Percent Base.
Must have met at least 90 percent of Contest Unit Base

Experience Factors
Contest Credits vary, based on the length of time a person has served as a Country Companies agent, as shown below. These factors will also impact the agency's Contest Credit totals.

Agent Experience (As of 12-1-1999)
Contest Credits Received
Basic Needs Agents
125% of Contest Credits Earned
0-12 months
120% of Contest Credits Earned
13-24 months
115% of Contest Credits Earned
25-36 months
110% of Contest Credits Earned
37-48 months
105% of Contest Credits Earned
More than 48 months
100% of Contest Credits Earned

THE BIG DANCE

THE BIG DANCE
That's what fans call the NCAA Division I tournament. And whether they say so or not, everyone who loves college basketball wants to make it there. Little else matters. Because regardless of the success a player, coach or team enjoys, they all dream of making it to 'the dance.'

It's a reward for a year's worth of focus and effort. It's about talent and heart and making sacrifices others did not. It's about doing what it takes to rise above the rest. It's about fulfilling a dream and earning the *National Champion's* ring.

This year, we're introducing our own version of "THE BIG DANCE." It, too, will reward focus, heart and sacrifice. It, too, will be about fulfilling dreams.

Are You Ready to Play?
At the end of each NCAA season, 64 teams are invited to 'the dance.' Once the tourney begins, the field quickly narrows. From 64 to 32, from 32 to the "Sweet Sixteen," "Elite Eight" and "Final Four." The battles end only after the *National Champion* has been crowned.

In our dance, agents and agencies will compete during a yearlong contest. At the conclusion, we will rank all agents and agencies based on their performance. The TOP 640 AGENTS AND 64 AGENCIES meeting our contest requirements will earn their invitation to THE BIG DANCE and participate in our NATIONAL TOURNAMENT. We'll host two very special ALL STAR TRIPS for all agents and managers meeting our midyear qualification requirements, too.

Here's Your Letter
We've attached your letter to this book, to help serve as a reminder of your goals during this contest. Each step of the way, from ALL STAR to THE BIG DANCE and beyond, we'll award a special pin to all that qualify. It's a mark of distinction shared by a select few...those who pay the price to be among the best.

Here's Your Playbook
This book contains everything you need to know about THE BIG DANCE. How the contest works. How to earn your invitation. And most importantly, all the great prizes you can win along the way if you've got what it takes to make it to the dance. *Interested?* Take a look inside to learn more.

DESIGN FIRM > Hand Made Group
ART DIRECTORS > Alessandro Esteri, Giona Maisrelli
DESIGNERS > Alessandro Esteri, Giona Maisrelli
ILLUSTRATOR/PHOTOGRAPHER > Alessandro Esteri
COPYWRITER > Verdiana Maggiorelli
CLIENT > Microtex S.P.A.
TOOLS (SOFTWARE/PLATFORM) > Apple, QuarkXPress, Freehand, Photoshop
PAPER STOCK > Zanders
PRINTING PROCESS > Printed in Pantone

DESIGN FIRM › Grant Design Collaborative
ILLUSTRATOR/PHOTOGRAPHER › Maria Robledo
CLIENT › JM Lynne Co., Inc.
TOOLS (SOFTWARE/PLATFORM) › Macintosh, QuarkXPress, Photoshop
PAPER STOCK › Cover—Mohawk Tomohawk New Smoke 65 lb. cover; text-Utopia 2
PRINTING PROCESS › Cover—foil Stamp with two PMS; text—6/6 with four-color and two PMS

a conscium business

RELIABLE TIMELY SECURE CONFIDENTIAL TRUSTWORTHY COLLABORATIVE INNOVATIVE EFFICIENT ACCURATE PROFESSIONAL EVOLUTIONARY ACCOMMODATING RELIABLE TIMELY REASONABLE SECURE CONFIDENTIAL TRUSTWORTHY INNOVATIVE

DESIGN FIRM > Michael Patrick Partners
ART DIRECTOR > Matt Sanders
DESIGNERS > Vonus D'amore, Stephanie West
COPYWRITER > Financialprinter.com

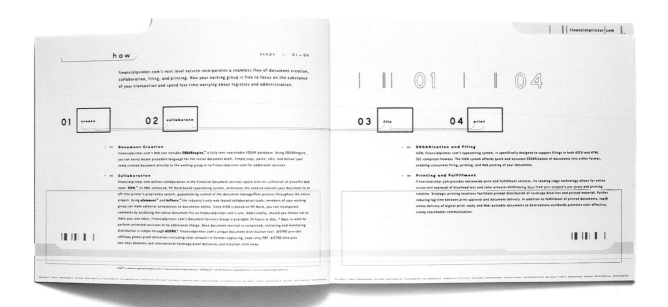

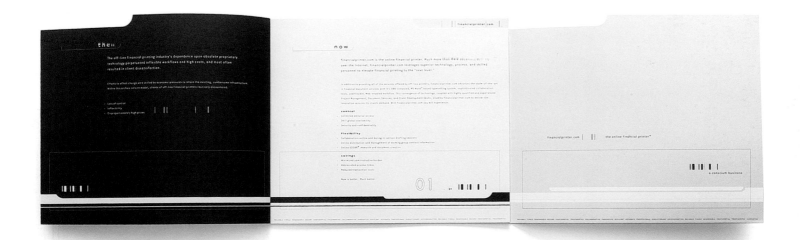

DESIGN FIRM > Michael Patrick Partners
ART DIRECTOR > Dan O'Brien
DESIGNER > Connie Hwang
ILLUSTRATOR/PHOTOGRAPHER > Various
COPYWRITER > Tim Peters
CLIENT > Chase H & Q
PAPER STOCK > Cornado, 100 lb. text, Fox River Company
PRINTER > Graphics Center

DESIGN FIRM > Michael Courtney Design
ART DIRECTORS > Mike Courtney, Scott Souchok
DESIGNERS > Mike Courtney, Scott Souchok
PHOTOGRAPHER > Stock, Kevin Latona
COPYWRITER > The Frause Group
CLIENT > Vulcan Northwest
TOOLS (SOFTWARE/PLATFORM) > Freehand, Photoshop
PAPER STOCK > Potlatch McCoy
PRINTING PROCESS > Four-color offset

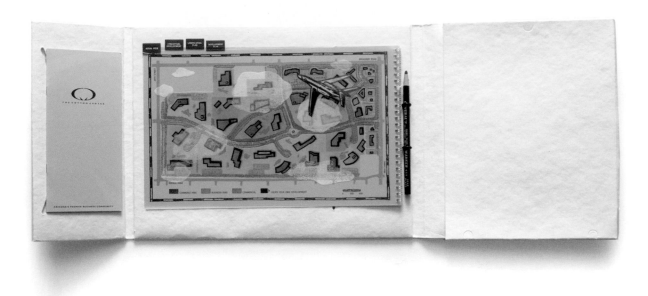

THE COTTON CENTER IS 280 ACRES OF
EXTRAORDINARY BUSINESS OPPORTUNITY.

STRATEGICALLY LOCATED LESS THAN FIVE MINUTES
FROM PHOENIX SKY HARBOR INTERNATIONAL
AIRPORT, THE COTTON CENTER PROVIDES
INCOMPARABLE ACCESS TO THE ENTIRE PHOENIX
METROPOLITAN AREA.

BECAUSE THE COTTON CENTER IS IN THE CENTER OF
THE REGION'S FREEWAY SYSTEM, MORE THAN 95% OF
THE POPULATION OF AMERICA'S SIXTH LARGEST CITY
LIVES WITHIN 40 MINUTES OF THE HEART OF
THE COTTON CENTER.

THE AFFLUENT AND FAST-GROWING COMMUNITIES OF
SCOTTSDALE, TEMPE, AHWATUKEE, CHANDLER,
GILBERT AND MESA ARE WITHIN 20 MINUTES OF
THE COTTON CENTER.

ARIZONA STATE UNIVERSITY, WITH ITS RENOWNED
UNDERGRADUATE AND GRADUATE SCHOOLS, RESEARCH
FACILITIES, BUSINESS INCUBATOR PROGRAMS AND
THINK-TANKS IS ONLY 25 BLOCKS AWAY. 19
ADDITIONAL INSTITUTIONS OF HIGHER LEARNING ARE
WITHIN 20 MINUTES.

THIS IS NOT YOUR TYPICAL COMMERCIAL REAL ESTATE.
THIS IS THE VERY DEFINITION OF A PREMIER
BUSINESS COMMUNITY.

DESIGN FIRM > After Hours Creative
ART DIRECTOR > After Hours Creative
DESIGNER > After Hours Creative
ILLUSTRATOR > Rick Allen
COPYWRITER > After Hours Creative
CLIENT > Cotton Center
TOOLS (SOFTWARE/PLATFORM) > Macintosh G4, Adobe Illustrator

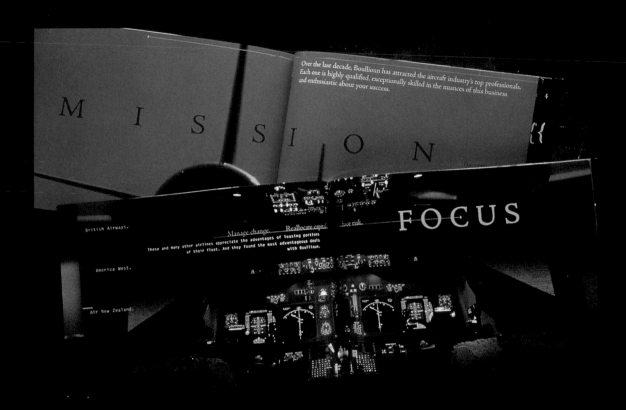

DESIGN FIRM > Hornall Anderson Design Works, Inc.
ART DIRECTORS > Jack Anderson, Katha Dalton
DESIGNERS > Katha Dalton, Ryan Wilderson, Belinda Bowling
PHOTOGRAPHERS > Boeing, West Stock, Tony Stone, Alan Abramowitz
COPYWRITER > John Koval
CLIENT > Boullioun Aviation Services
TOOLS (SOFTWARE/PLATFORM) > QuarkXPress
PAPER STOCK > McCoy, Strathmore

Every year over a million Silicon Valley residents turn off their computers and go in search of adventure and romance.

They go on vacation. To Europe. Mexico. Hawaii. The Caribbean. And every other corner of the globe.

This large number of travelers, and their passion for the road, makes Santa Clara County the most lucrative travel market in Northern California.

DESIGN FIRM › Cox Design
ART DIRECTOR › Randy Cox
DESIGNER › Randy Cox
COPYWRITER › Mike Furnary
CLIENT › San Jose Mercury News
TOOLS (SOFTWARE/PLATFORM) › Photoshop, QuarkXPress, Macintosh
PAPER STOCK › French
PRINTING PROCESS › Offset

adventure

culture

romance

history

1999 Special Advertising Features of the San Jose Mercury News Sunday Travel Section

DESIGN FIRM › Hand Made Group
ART DIRECTORS › Alessandro Esteri, Giona Maisrelli
DESIGNERS › Alessandro Esteri, Giona Maisrelli
ILLUSTRATOR/PHOTOGRAPHER › Alessandro Esteri
COPYWRITER › Verdiana Maggiorelli
CLIENT › Tessile Fiorentina
TOOLS (SOFTWARE/PLATFORM) › QuarkXpress, Photoshop
PAPER STOCK › Zanders
PRINTING PROCESS › Printed in Pantone

DESIGN FIRM > Gee + Chung Design
ART DIRECTOR > Earl Gee
DESIGNERS > Earl Gee, Qui Tong
PHOTOGRAPHER > Stock
COPYWRITERS > Tracy Harvey, Susan Berman
CLIENT > Netigy Corporation
TOOLS (SOFTWARE/PLATFORM) > QuarkXPress, Adobe Illustrator, Photoshop
PAPER STOCK > Springhill SBS C25 24 pt., Appleton Utopia, 65 lb. cover
PRINTING PROCESS > Offset lithography, die-cut cover

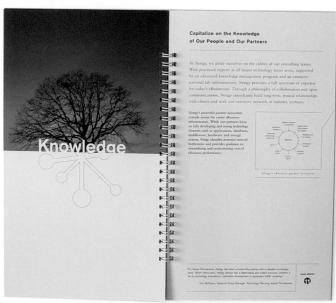

DESIGN FIRM > The Bonsey Design Partnership
ART DIRECTOR > Chris Lee
DESIGNER > Damien Thomasz
PHOTOGRAPHERS > Andrew Hun, Alex Ow
COPYWRITER > Jane Cotter
CLIENT > Transtel Engineering
TOOLS (SOFTWARE/PLATFORM) > Macintosh, Freehand, Photoshop
PAPER STOCK > Matt art card
PRINTING PROCESS > Five-color plus one special

DESIGN FIRM > Fossil
ART DIRECTORS > Tim Hale, Stephen Zhang
DESIGNER > Stephen Zhang
ILLUSTRATORS > Ellen Tanner, Paula Wallace, John Vineyard, Jennifer Burk, Andrea Haynes
PHOTOGRAPHER > Dave McCormack
CLIENT > Fossil
TOOLS (SOFTWARE/PLATFORM) > QuarkXPress, Photoshop, Illustrator, Macintosh G3, Power PC
PAPER STOCK > Fox River Protera
PRINTING PROCESS > Four-color offset

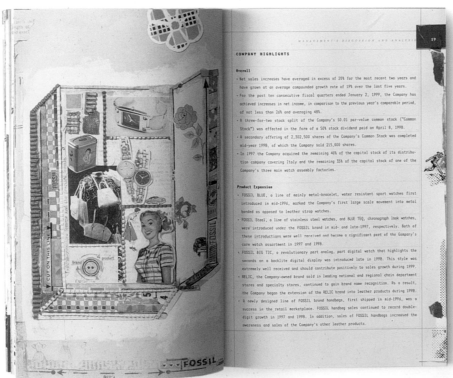

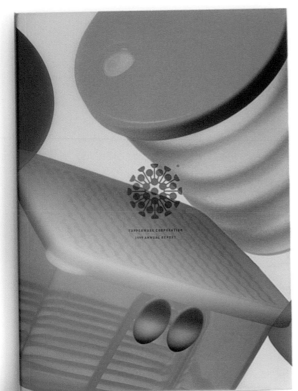

DESIGN FIRM › SamataMason, Inc.
ART DIRECTOR › Greg Samata
DESIGNER › Steve Kull
PHOTOGRAPHERS › Sandro, Marc Norberg, Mark Craig
COPYWRITER › Laurence Pearson
CLIENT › Tupperware Corporation
TOOLS (SSOFTWARE/PLATFORM) › QuarkXPress, Macintosh
PAPER STOCK › Fox River, Coronado Vellum, Fox River Sundance, Canson satin
PRINTING PROCESS › Offset, sheet fed

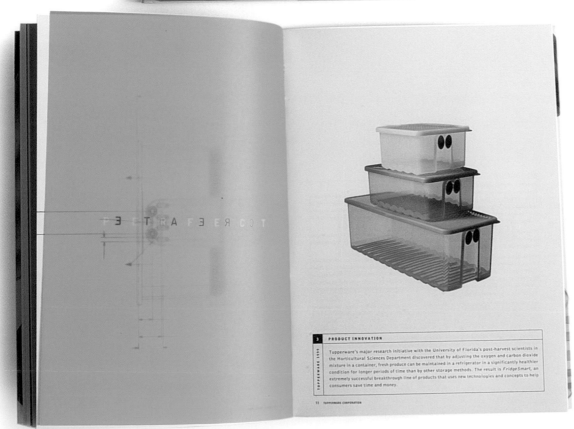

3 PRODUCT INNOVATION

Tupperware's major research initiative with the University of Florida's post-harvest scientists in the Horticultural Sciences Department discovered that by adjusting the oxygen and carbon dioxide mixture in a container, fresh produce can be maintained in a refrigerator in a significantly healthier condition for longer periods of time than by other storage methods. The result is *FridgeSmart*, an extremely successful breakthrough line of products that uses new technologies and concepts to help consumers save time and money.

13 TUPPERWARE CORPORATION

DESIGN FIRM > Bloch + Coulter Design Group

ART DIRECTORS > Hollie Hory, Thomas Bloch, Ellie Young Sutt

DESIGNERS > Hollie Hory, Thomas Bloch, Ellie Young Sutt

PHOTOGRAPHER > Jerry Garns

COPYWRITER > Paul Losie

CLIENT > Amwest Insurance Group, Inc.

TOOLS (SOFTWARE/PLATFORM) > Macintosh, QuarkXPress, Photoshop, Illustrator

PAPER STOCK > Editorial: Potlatch Karma 100 lb. text; Flysheet: French Parchtone cream 60 lb. text, Financial: Beckett embossed enhanced silk 80 lb., text

PRINTING PROCESS > All but cover sheet fed, hand bound with Acco fastener

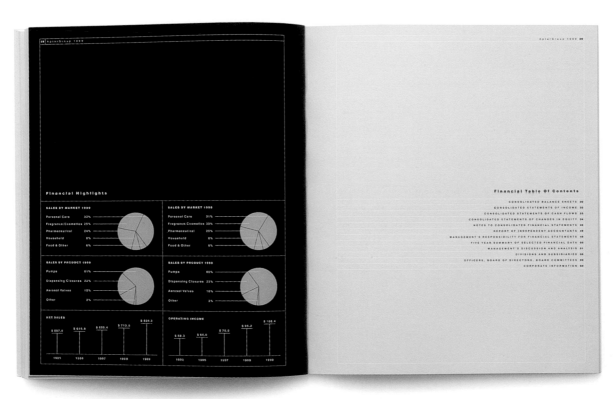

DESIGN FIRM > SamataMason, Inc.
ART DIRECTORS > Pat & Greg Samata
DESIGNER > Kevin Krueger
PHOTOGRAPHER > Sandro
CLIENT > Aptar Group
TOOLS (SOFTWARE/PLATFORM) > QuarkXPress, Macintosh
PAPER STOCK > Appleton—coated Utopia one, dull; Monadnock Aastrolite vellum
PRINTING PROCESS > Offset, sheet fed

DESIGN FIRM › Edelman Public Relations Worldwide

ART DIRECTOR › Mary Ackerly

DESIGNERS › Rosanne Kang, Lana Le

PHOTOGRAPHERS › Josef Astor, Whitney Cox, Doug Levere, Peter Loppacher, William Vasquez

COPYWRITER › Various

CLIENT › Barnes and Noble

TOOLS (SOFTWARE/PLATFORM) › QuarkXpress, Adobe Illustrator, Macintosh

PAPER STOCK › Mohawk 50/10

PRINTING PROCESS › Offset lithography

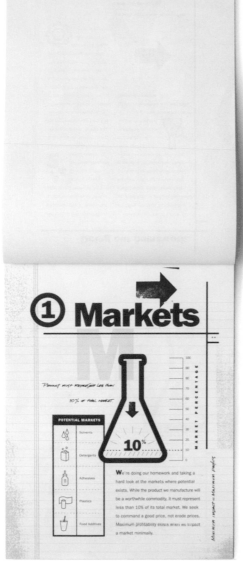

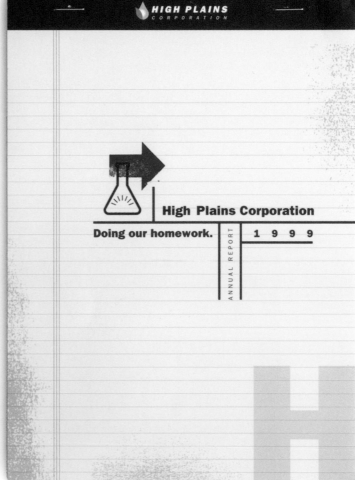

DESIGN FIRM › Greteman Group
ART DIRECTORS › Sonia Greteman, James Strange
DESIGNER › James Strange
PHOTOGRAPHER › Steve Rasmussen
COPYWRITERS › Deanna Harms, Raleigh Drennon
CLIENT › High Plains
TOOLS (SOFTWARE/PLATFORM) › Freehand
PAPER STOCK › Productolith

DESIGN FIRM › Intraware, Inc. (Creative Services Group)
ART DIRECTOR › Rudolph O'Meara
DESIGNER › Rudolph O'Meara
ILLUSTRATOR/PHOTOGRAPHER › Stock
COPYWRITERS › Jon Rant, Thea Gray
CLIENT › Intraware, Inc.
TOOLS (SOFTWARE/PLATFORM) › QuarkXPress, Adobe Photoshop, Illustrator
PAPER STOCK › 80 lb. cool white Mohawk, 27 lb. yellow chromatica

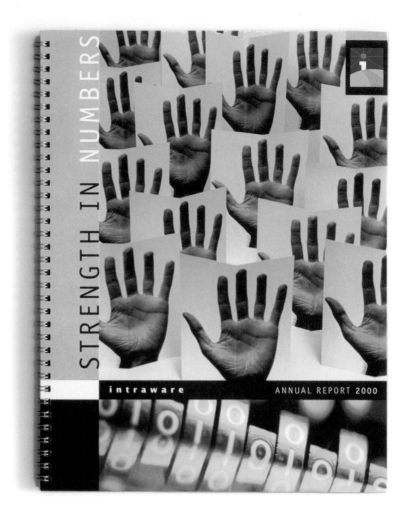

One of the reasons that Intraware's customer base grew exponentially over the course of the last year was because of our success in increasing the products and vendors available through our online procurement services. At the close of the fiscal year we sold and supported over 1,500 software and courseware product lines available from more than 60 vendor partners. The software partners included such key FY2000 additions as Hewlett-Packard, Novell, Computer Associates, Vignette, and BEA. Information vendors such as Gartner, Aberdeen Group, Books24x7.com, and Business Week Online, as well as training courseware providers SmartForce and Paragon, have also become Intraware partners in the past fiscal year.

PARTNERSHIPS

We have also increased the number of companies licensing our software management services for use by their own customers. New partners such as PeopleSoft, Commerce One, E.piphany, and Interwoven are now able to reduce costs and offer their customers better service through software update notifications and online access to updates and release archives. The more partners we add, the more the market becomes aware of Intraware's technological expertise—generating the critical mass necessary to strengthen our position as the leading IT e-marketplace. Matchmaker, market maker; with Intraware in the middle, the IT puzzle becomes far less complicated for enterprise users and vendors alike.

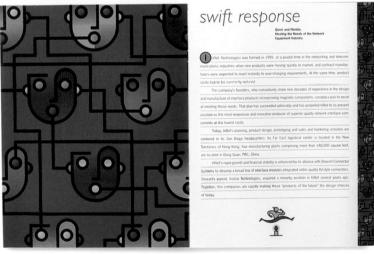

DESIGN FIRM > Lorenz Advertising
ART DIRECTOR > Arne Ratermanis
DESIGNER > Arne Ratermanis
ILLUSTRATORS/PHOTOGRAPHERS > Arne Ratermanis, Michael Balderas
COPYWRITER > Carm Greco
CLIENT > InNet Technologies
TOOLS (SOFTWARE/PLATFORM) > QuarkXPress, Illustrator, Macintosh
PAPER STOCK > Potlatch McCoy Gloss
PRINTING PROCESS > Four-color litho with dull and gloss varnish; embossed cover

CONNOISSEUR

PRODUCT **BROCHURES**

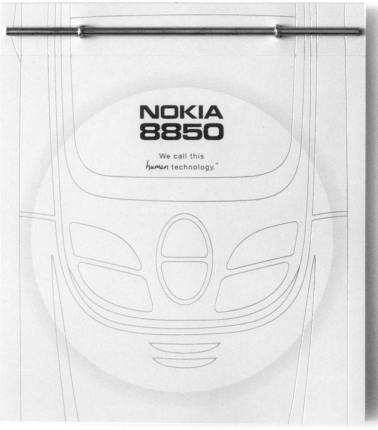

A craftsman's pride. An object of desire. A very personal pleasure. Introducing the Nokia 8850.

DESIGN FIRM > 141 Singapore Pte Ltd.
ART DIRECTOR > Doris Hiw
DESIGNER > Doris Hiw
ILLUSTRATOR/PHOTOGRAPHER > David Allan Brandt
COPYWRITER > Kok Chin Yin
CLIENT > Nokia Pte Ltd.
PAPER STOCK > 250 gsm Eagle Silohuette premium matt, 155 gsm GSK transparent natural
PRINTING PROCESS > Two-sided, 6c x 7c solid varnish, 1c x 0c tracing, matt silver stamping

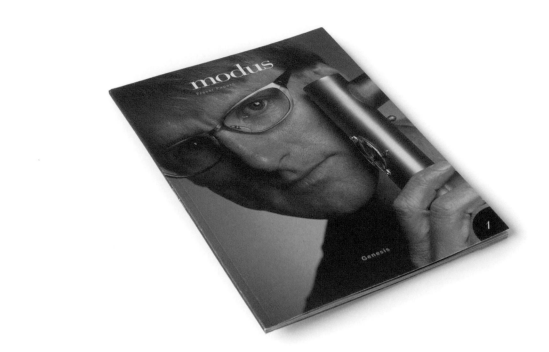

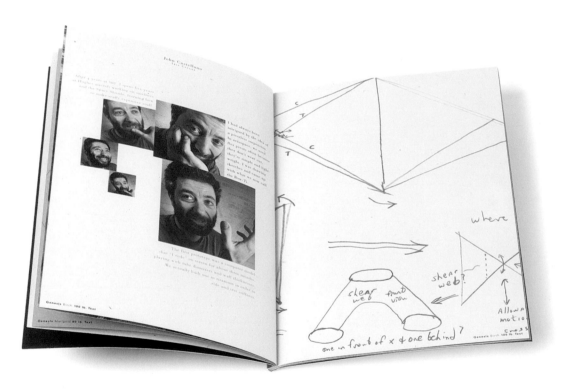

DESIGN FIRM > Douglas Joseph Partners

ART DIRECTORS > Scott Lambert, Doug Joseph

DESIGNER > Scott Lambert

ILLUSTRATORS > Juliette Borda, Eddie Guy

PHOTOGRAPHERS > Dave Teel, Jeff Zaruba, Rick Chou, Eric Tucker, Scott Lambert, Diana Koenigsberg

COPYWRITER > Delphine Hirasuna

CLIENT > Fraser Papers

TOOLS (SOFTWARE/PLATFORM) > QuarkXPress on Macintosh

PAPER STOCK > Fraser genesis, synergy, passport

Uphill and downhill riding are separate experiences.

Uphill you can have discussions, think about things.

Downhill is a real "be here now" experience; it clears your brain out.

If you don't, you crash. I love that feeling of swooping through things, leaning into the corners, getting into the groove.

Genesis Marigold 80 lb. Text

Genesis Birch 100 lb. Text

Genesis Birch 100 lb. Text

Genesis Birch 100 lb. Text

Genesis Birch 100 lb. Text

DESIGN FIRM › Emery Vincent Design
ART DIRECTOR › Garry Emery
DESIGNER › Emery Vincent Design
CLIENT › Maxton Fox
TOOLS (SOFTWARE/PLATFORM) › QuarkXPress, Illustrator, Photoshop

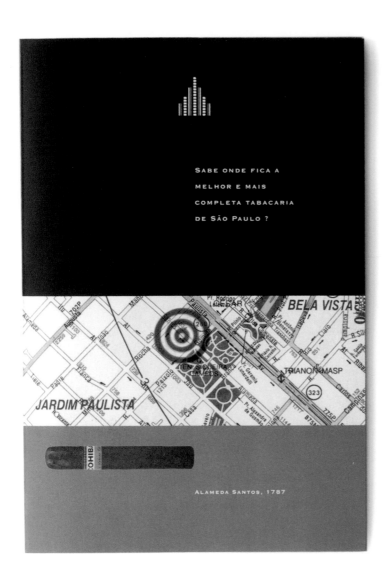

DESIGN FIRM › José J. Dias da S. Junior
ART DIRECTOR › José J. Dias da S. Junior
DESIGNER › José J. Dias da S. Junior
CLIENT › The Cigar Place
TOOLS (SOFTWARE/PLATFORM) › Photoshop, Corel Draw, Page Maker for PC
PAPER STOCK › Unpolished couche

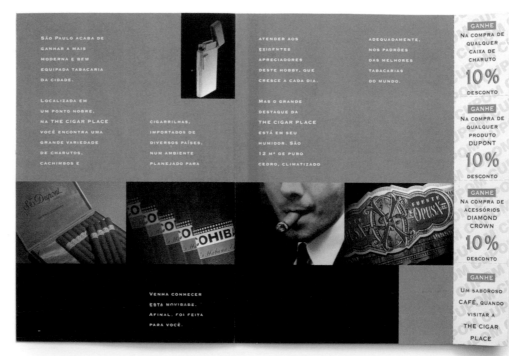

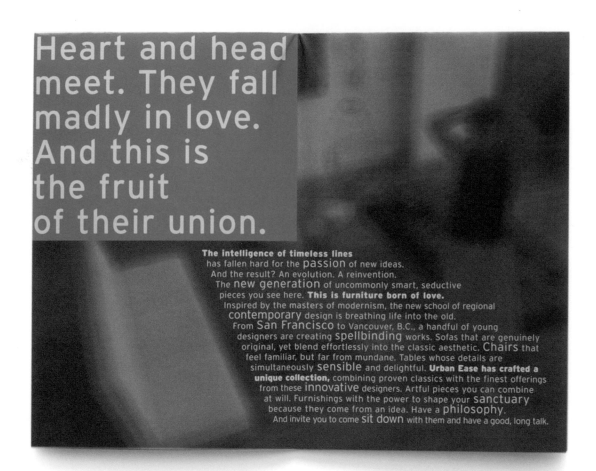

Heart and head meet. They fall madly in love. And this is the fruit of their union.

The intelligence of timeless lines has fallen hard for the passion of new ideas. And the result? An evolution. A reinvention. The new generation of uncommonly smart, seductive pieces you see here. **This is furniture born of love.** Inspired by the masters of modernism, the new school of regional contemporary design is breathing life into the old. From San Francisco to Vancouver, B.C., a handful of young designers are creating spellbinding works. Sofas that are genuinely original, yet blend effortlessly into the classic aesthetic. Chairs that feel familiar, but far from mundane. Tables whose details are simultaneously sensible and delightful. **Urban Ease has crafted a unique collection,** combining proven classics with the finest offerings from these innovative designers. Artful pieces you can combine at will. Furnishings with the power to shape your sanctuary because they come from an idea. Have a philosophy. And invite you to come sit down with them and have a good, long talk.

DESIGN FIRM › Giorgio Davanzo Design
ART DIRECTOR › Giorgio Davanzo
DESIGNER › Giorgio Davanzo
ILLUSTRATOR/PHOTOGRAPHER › Various
COPYWRITER › Mary LaCoste
CLIENT › Urban Ease
TOOLS (SOFTWARE/PLATFORM) › QuarkXPress 4.1, Photoshop 5.5, Illustrator 8.0 for Macintosh
PAPER STOCK › Hammermill via colors Sunflower
PRINTING PROCESS › Offset, two PMS colors

and does it work...?

— **Jackie Cooper** 1993

systematic reflections on a safe future

do create

DESIGN FIRM › Kesselskramer
ART DIRECTOR › Erik Kessels
DESIGNER › Karen Heuter
ILLUSTRATORS/PHOTOGRAPHERS › Stang, Bianca Pilet
COPYWRITER › David Bell
CLIENT › Do
TOOLS (SOFTWARE/PLATFORM) › QuarkXPress, Apple Macintosh
PAPER STOCK/PRINTING PROCESS › Cyclus print
PRINTING PROCESS › Offset, sheet

DESIGN FIRM > Zappata Diseñadores S.C.
ART DIRECTOR > Ibo Angulo
DESIGNER > Ibo Angulo
PHOTOGRAPHER > Ricardo Trabulsi
CLIENT > Laura Lavalle
TOOLS (SOFTWARE/PLATFORM) > Photoshop, Freehand
PRINTING PROCESS > Offset

DESIGN FIRM > Zappata Diseñadores S.C.
ART DIRECTOR > Ibo Angulo
DESIGNER > Ibo Angulo
COPYWRITER > © Disney/Pixar
CLIENT > Cupa Chups
TOOLS (SOFTWARE/PLATFORM) > Adobe Illustrator
PRINTING PROCESS > Offset

STINGER

PURE FAST. PURE RACE.

If heart rates, hill intervals and dirt monitoring are the staple of your mountain biking then the STINGER is for you. With it's patented super rigid shock mounting, the shortest distance from the rear axle to the shock mount is obtained. This allows for lighter construction and the most laterally rigid shock frame available, making this the only ultra light frame you want to be hammering out the miles on. We use Easton Elite tubing on the top and down tubes, and custom drawn seat tube and stays for maximum rigidity and low weight. The shock is a custom version of the Fox Float R with dampening adjustment. With the perfect pivot placement resulting from 7 years of frame design experience a lock-out shock is not necessary. Just set the air pressure and hammer! Designed around cross country racing forks with 60mm of travel.

2.8" travel, 70.5 head, 73.5 seat
14, 15.5, 17, 18, 19.5

O2

SERIOUSLY LIGHT ROCKER...

The O2 is the lightest linkage frame on the market." If you are a cross country rider and occasional racer who doesn't want a lot of weight in order to have the benefits of a linkage design, this is it. The O2 offers 3.1" of wheel travel with the super light Fox Air Float R C keeping the suspension stiction free and adjustable. We use Easton Elite tubing on the top and down tubes, and custom drawn seat tube and stays for maximum rigidity and low weight. The O2 is very light, yet it offers enough travel to satisfy most riders. It will make the epic days and long climbs less painful and the O2 has been a hit with the high mileage addicts. By design it leans toward the Stinger side of the family, giving a crisp responsive ride. "With grease fittings, seals, replaceable d-hanger & multi brake options.

3.1" travel, 70.5 head, 73.5 seat
14, 15.5, 17, 18, 19.5, 21

BURNER XCE

ULTIMATE FUN BIKE

This is the all terrain fun bike for the toughest rider in the world. The world renowned Burner is the ideal trail bike for the heavier and/or aggressive cross country rider. The plush 4 inches of wheel travel is for the rider who demands the ultimate in comfort and control. Our proven 4 bar linkage system ensures reliability and maximum rigidity. The XCE comes equipped with a FOX Coil Over Vanilla RC with compression and rebound controls. The pivot locations are perfect for your type of riding. It will not partially fade out when you are wrestling over that rock pile, and it doesn't bob noticeably when hammering the smoother sections. If you challenge yourself with the toughest climbs and descend rocky trails and screaming fire roads, the XCE will keep you smiling hour after hour. The XCE is designed around a single crown fork with 100mm of travel to maintain proper geometry.

4.0" travel, 70 head, 73.5 seat
15, 16 & 18, 19.5, 21

RFX

SICK DROPS? NO PROBLEM.

This is a free ride frame, period. We applied the lessons we learned on the DH race circuit to this frame so you can go for the biggest wheelie-drops and G-outs that your body can take. With 27 speed capability and optimized pivot locations, after bombing to the bottom of the mountain you can actually ride back up. The RFX enjoys 6 inches of wheel travel controlled by a Fox Vanilla RC reservoir shock with compression and rebound damping. For proper balance and geometry, a fork with 150mm of wheel travel should be used, a rocker is available for 5" of travel to match the 5" travel forks on the market. If you are a free rider seeking the finest in design and construction, matching corners close to the ride or quality of the RFX.

6" travel, 69 head, 73.5 seat
15.5, 17, 18, 19.5, 21

DESIGN FIRM > Damion Hickman Design
ART DIRECTOR > Damion Hickman
DESIGNER > Damion Hickman
ILLUSTRATOR/PHOTOGRAPHER > Greg Nesler
COPYWRITER > David Turner
CLIENT > Turner Bicycles
TOOLS (SOFTWARE/PLATFORM) > Illustrator

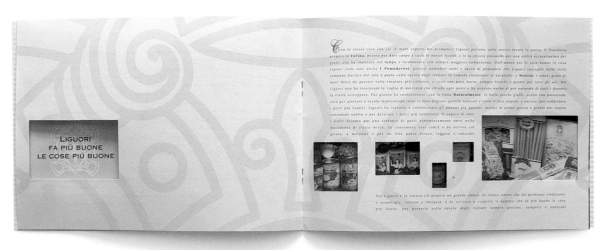

DESIGN FIRM ❯ R & M Associati Grafici
ART DIRECTORS ❯ Fontanella, Di Somma, Cesar
DESIGNERS ❯ Fontanella, Di Somma, Cesar
PHOTOGRAPHER ❯ Franco Gargiulo
CLIENT ❯ Pastificio Liguori
TOOLS (SOFTWARE/PLATFORM) ❯ Adobe Illustrator 8.0
PRINTING PROCESS ❯ Offset

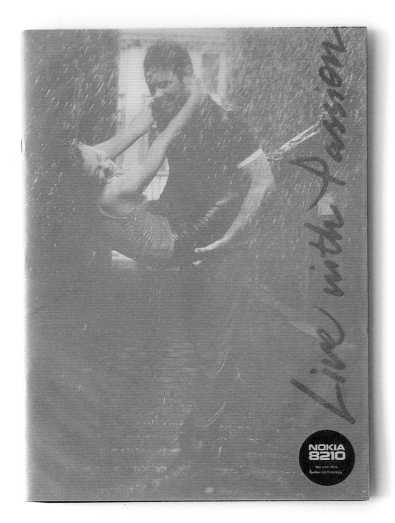

DESIGN FIRM › 141 Singapore Pte Ltd.
ART DIRECTOR › Winnie Lee
DESIGNER › Wnnie Lee
ILLUSTRATORS/PHOTOGRAPHERS › Tomek and Eryk Photography Pty
COPYWRITER › Kok Chin Yin
CLIENT › Nokia Pte Ltd.
PAPER STOCK › Cover–112gsm GSK transparent paper; text–210 gsm Eagle Silhouette matt artcard
PRINTING PROCESS › Cover–3c x 0c; text–5c x 5c, solid matt artcard

DESIGN FIRM > Palmquist Creative
ART DIRECTORS > Kurt Palmquist, Kelly Bellcour
DESIGNERS > Kurt Palmquist, Kelly Bellcour
PHOTOGRAPHERS > Rob Wilke, Denver Bryan
COPYWRITER > Client
CLIENT > Field & Stream
TOOLS (SOFTWARE/PLATFORM) > Adobe Pagemaker, Illustrator, Macintosh
PAPER STOCK/PRINTING PROCESS > Frostbrite, 80 lb. book, white

DESIGN FIRM > Alternatives
ART DIRECTOR > Julie Koch-Beinke
DESIGNER > Julie Koch-Beinke
ILLUSTRATOR/PHOTOGRAPHER > Various
CLIENT > Sungold Eyewear
TOOLS (SOFTWARE/PLATFORM) > Illustrator, Macintosh
PAPER STOCK > Metallic pearl white for cover, 100 lb. gloss cover
PRINTING PROCESS > Four-color process

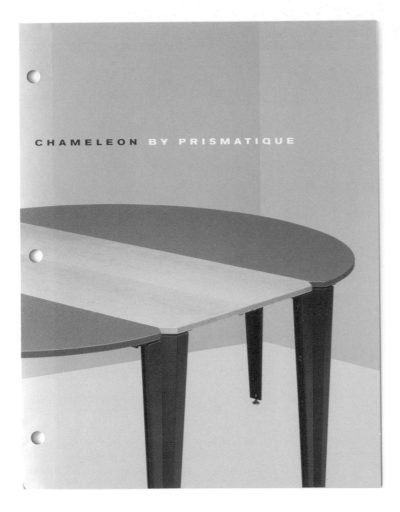

DESIGN FIRM > Dinnick & Howells
ART DIRECTOR > Jonathan Howells
DESIGNERS > Dwayne Dobson, Tracey Hanson
CLIENT > Prismatique
TOOLS (SOFTWARE/PLATFORM) > Macintosh G3, Illustrator, Photoshop

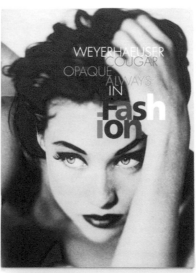

DESIGN FIRM > Sibley Peteet Design
ART DIRECTOR > Don Sibley
DESIGNERS > Don Sibley, Donna Aldridge
PHOTOGRAPHERS > Various
COPYWRITER > Don Sibley
CLIENT > Weyerhaeuser Paper
TOOLS (SOFTWARE/PLATFORM) > QuarkXPress, Macintosh
PAPER STOCK > Weyerhaeuser Cougar opaque

DESIGN FIRM › Creative Conspiracy, Inc.
ART DIRECTOR › Kris Hickcox
DESIGNER › Kris Hickcox
ILLUSTRATOR/PHOTOGRAPHER › Neil Hannum
CLIENT › Screaming Rhino Gift Market
TOOLS (SOFTWARE/PLATFORM) › QuarkXPress, Illustrator, Photoshop
PAPER STOCK/PRINTING PROCESS › Catalog: 80 lb. McCoy—text; 4/4 with bleeds—cover.
Env: 80 lb. Gilbert Voice in Rye

DESIGN FIRM > Arias Associates

ART DIRECTOR > Mauricio Arias

DESIGNER > Mauricio Arias

ILLUSTRATORS/PHOTOGRAPHERS > Mike Halbert, Stefano Massei

COPYWRITER > Pottery Barn

CLIENT > Pottery Barn

TOOLS (SOFTWARE/PLATFORM) > QuarkXPress, Photoshop

PAPER STOCK > Champion Benefit, Mohawk superfine

PRINTING PROCESS > Lithography and letterpress

DESIGN FIRM > Giorgio Rocco Communications
ART DIRECTOR > Giorgio Rocco
DESIGNER > Giorgio Rocco
ILLUSTRATOR/PHOTOGRAPHER > Archives INDA
COPYWRITER > Elisabetta Campo
CLIENT > INDA spa, Italy
TOOLS (SOFTWARE/PLATFORM) > Macintosh, Photoshop, Freehand
PAPER STOCK > Burgo
PRINTING PROCESS > Four-color offset

DESIGN FIRM > Kan & Lau Design Consultants
ART DIRECTORS > Kan Tai-keung, Veronica Cheung, Mak Tsing Kuoh
DESIGNERS > Kan Tai-keung, Veronica Cheung, Mak Tsing Kuoh
COMPUTER ILLUSTRATOR > Ng Cheuk Bong
CLIENT > Rolex (HK) Ltd

DESIGN FIRM › Hand Made Group
ART DIRECTORS › Alessandro Esteri, Giona Maisrelli
DESIGNERS › Alessandro Esteri, Giona Maisrelli
ILLUSTRATOR/PHOTOGRAPHER › Alessandro Esteri
COPYWRITER › Verdiana Maggiorelli
CLIENT › Marco Pierguidi
TOOLS (SOFTWARE/PLATFORM) › QuarkXPress, Photoshop
PAPER STOCK › Garda
PRINTING PROCESS › Four-color

DESIGN FIRM > Oden Marketing and Design
CREATIVE DIRECTOR > Bret Terwilleger
DESIGNER > Michael Guthrie
ILLUSTRATOR > Michael Koelsch
PENCILS > Dean Zachary
COPYWRITER > Henry Ellis
CLIENT > Accent Opaque
PAPER STOCK > Williamson

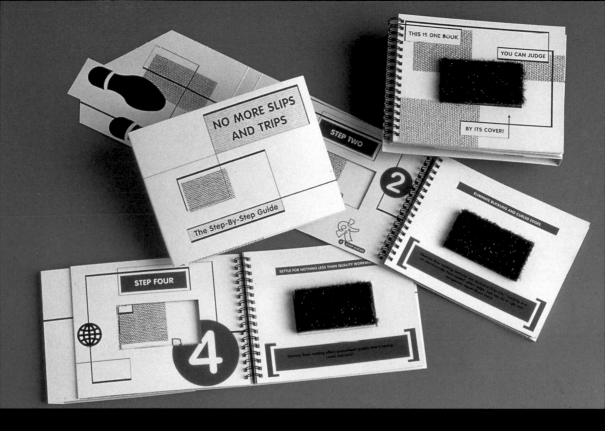

DESIGN FIRM > Sayles Graphic Design
ART DIRECTOR > John Sayles
DESIGNER > John Sayles
ILLUSTRATOR > John Sayles
COPYWRITER > Wendy Lyons
CLIENT > Sbemco International
TOOLS (SOFTWARE/PLATFORM) > QuarkXPress, Illustrator, Macintosh

DESIGN FIRM › Fossil, Inc.
ART DIRECTORS › Tim Hale, Hans Dorsinville
DESIGNER › Brad Bollinger
PHOTOGRAPHER › Dave McCormick
COPYWRITER › Kathleen Boyes
CLIENT › DKNY Watches
TOOLS (SOFTWARE/PLATFORM) › QuarkXPress 4.0, Photoshop 4.0, Illustrator 8.0, Apple Macintosh G3
PAPER STOCK › Text pages: Bravo matte book, acetate; Cover: Lucence 36 lb.

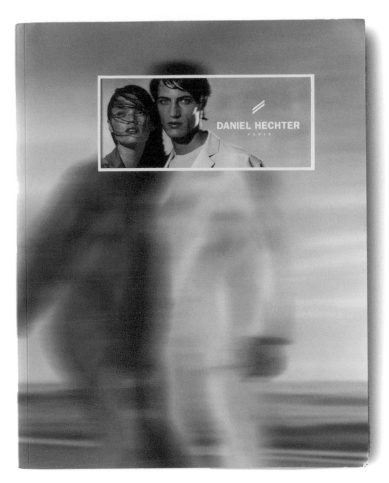

DESIGN FIRM › Hohenhorst Advertising Agency
ART DIRECTOR › Knut Ettling
DESIGNER › Knut Ettling
ILLUSTRATORS/PHOTOGRAPHERS › Michael Williams, Kristian Rahtsen
COPYWRITERS › Birgid Rudolf, Martina Wilde
CLIENT › Daniel Hechter
TOOLS (SOFTWARE/PLATFORM) › QuarkXPress

DESIGN FIRM › Greteman Group
ART DIRECTORS › Sonia Greteman, James Strange
DESIGNERS › James Strange, Craig Tomson
COPYWRITER › Raleigh Drennon
CLIENT › Flexjet
TOOLS (SOFTWARE/PLATFORM) › Freehand
PAPER STOCK › Gloss enamel Carolina C2S

DESIGN FIRM > Gardner Design
ART DIRECTORS > Bill Gardner, Brian Miller, Travis Brown
DESIGNER > Travis Brown
PHOTOGRAPHER > Paul Chauncey
COPYWRITER > John Brown
CLIENT > Excel
TOOLS (SOFTWARE/PLATFORM) > Freehand, Photoshop
PAPER STOCK > Four-color

DESIGN FIRM › Sackett Design Associates
ART DIRECTOR › Mark Sackett
DESIGNERS › James Sakamoto, Wendy Wood, George White
PHOTOGRAPHER › Robert Cardin
COPYWRITER › Bill Bisesto
CLIENT › Spark Online
TOOLS (SOFTWARE/PLATFORM) › Adobe Illustrator, Photoshop, QuarkXPress
PAPER STOCK › Potlatch McCoy silk 80 lb. cover brochures and 120 lb. cover folder

DESIGN FIRM › Pepe Gimeno - Proyecto Gráfico

ART DIRECTOR › Pepe Gimeno

DESIGNER › José P. Gil

CLIENT › International Furniture Fair of Valencia. cDIM

TOOLS (SOFTWARE/PLATFORM) › Freehand 8.0

PRINTING PROCESS › Offset

Vegetables are always
on our mind.

DESIGN FIRM › Lorenz Advertising
ART DIRECTOR › Glen Miranda
DESIGNER › Glen Miranda
ILLUSTRATORS/PHOTOGRAPHERS › Dan Thoner, various photographers
COPYWRITER › Carm Greco
CLIENT › Enza Zaden North America
TOOLS (SOFTWARE/PLATFORM) › QuarkXPress, Photoshop, Macintosh
PAPER STOCK › Simpson evergreen cord
PRINTING PROCESS › Five-color lithography

We've come a long way in this business...
all the way from Holland.

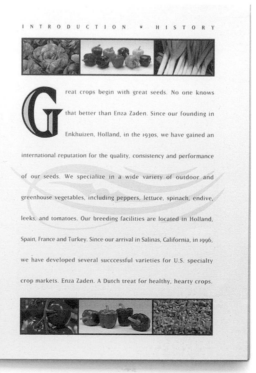

Great crops begin with great seeds. No one knows that better than Enza Zaden. Since our founding in Enkhuizen, Holland, in the 1930s, we have gained an international reputation for the quality, consistency and performance of our seeds. We specialize in a wide variety of outdoor and greenhouse vegetables, including peppers, lettuce, spinach, endive, leeks, and tomatoes. Our breeding facilities are located in Holland, Spain, France and Turkey. Since our arrival in Salinas, California, in 1996, we have developed several succcessful varieties for U.S. specialty crop markets. Enza Zaden. A Dutch treat for healthy, hearty crops.

DESIGNFIRM > Lee Reedy Creative
ART DIRECTOR > Lee Reedy
DESIGNER > Heather Haworth
ILLUSTRATORS/PHOTOGRAPHERS > Bruce Wolf, Marshal Safron, Michael Peck
COPYWRITER > Carol Parsons
CLIENT > Hunter Douglas
TOOLS (SOFTWARE/PLATFORM) > QuarkXPress
PAPER STOCK > McCoy, laminated and U.V. coated

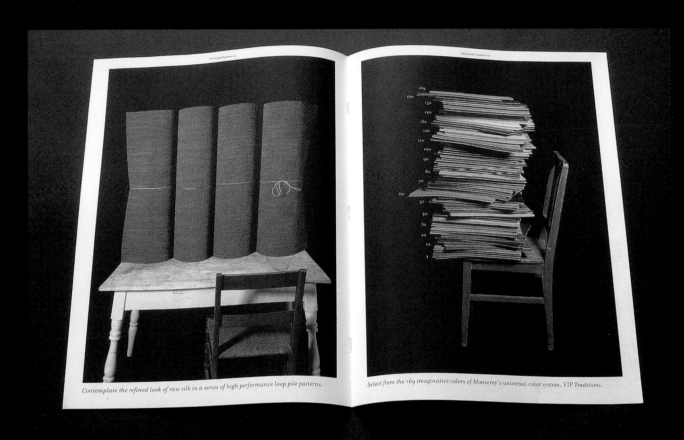

Contemplate the refined look of raw silk in a series of high performance loop pile patterns.

Select from the 169 imaginative colors of Monterey's universal color system. VIP Traditions.

DESIGN FIRM › Grant Design Collaborative

ILLUSTRATOR/PPHOTOGRAPHER › Geof Kern

CLIENT › Monterey Carpets

TOOLS (SOFTWARE/PLATFORM) › Macintosh, QuarkXPress, Photoshop

PAPER STOCK/PRINTING PROCESS › Cougar opaque 80 lb.
text smooth, 6/6

PRINTING PROCESS › Four-color, PMS, spot varnish

DESIGN FIRM › Burrows

ART DIRECTOR › Reg Malin

DESIGNER › Reg Malin

ILLUSTRATOR/PHOTOGRAPHER › John Cox

COPYWRITER › Joan Dance

CLIENT › Lincoln Mercury

TOOLS (SOFTWARE/PLATFORM) › QuarkXPress, Adobe Illustrator, Photoshop, Apple Power G3

PAPER STOCK › Potlatch McCoy silk

PRINTING PROCESS › Seven-color (three specials), varnish,
spot U.V. printed on a 40-inch Komori press in a single pass in line

DESIGN FIRM > Morla Design

ART DIRECTOR > Jennifer Morla

DESIGNERS > Jennifer Morla, Angela Williams

PHOTOGRAPHER > Jock McDonald

COPYWRITER > Penny Benda

CLIENT > Levi Strauss & Co.

TOOLS (SOFTWARE/PLATFORM) > QuarkXPress

PAPER STOCK > S.D. Warren Company Opus dull 80 lb. cover

PRINTING PROCESS > three-fourths-inch die cut holes on cover

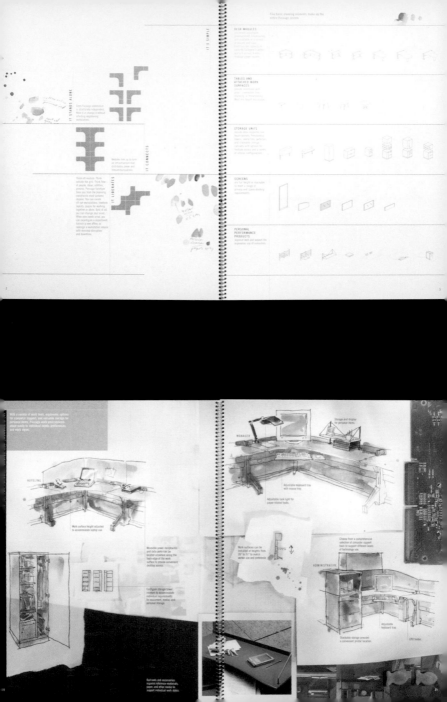

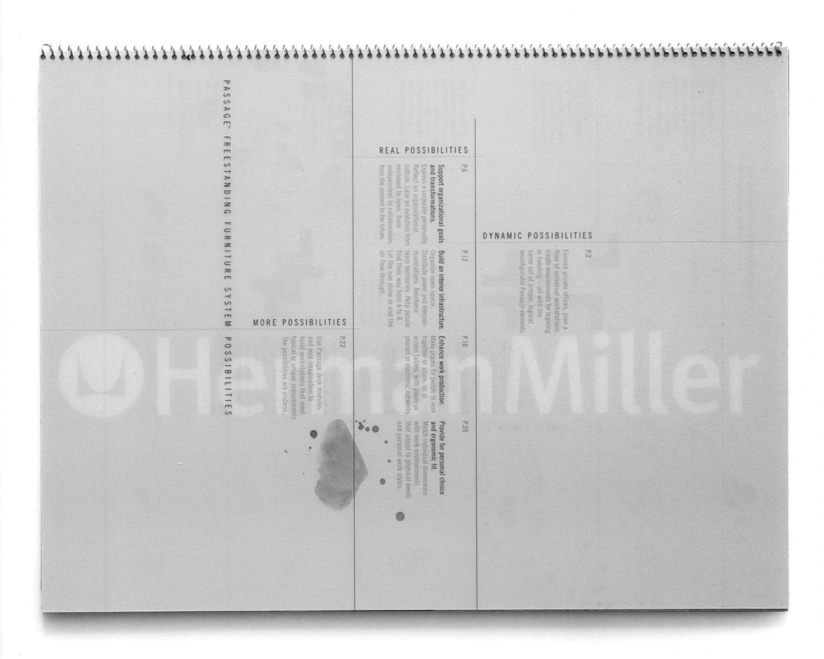

DESIGN FIRM > BBK Studio
ART DIRECTOR > Kevin Budelmann
DESIGNER > Alison Popp
ILLUSTRATORS > Linda Nelson, Mark Schlutt, Kurt Gould
PHOTOGRAPHERS > Nick Merrick, Bob Neumann, Dave Wolters, Susan Carr
COPYWRITER > Deb Wierenga
CLIENT > Herman Miller
TOOLS (SOFTWARE/PLATFORM) > QuarkXPress, Freehand
PAPER STOCK > Nekoosa Solutions and plastic

DESIGN FIRM › Fitch
ART DIRECTORS › Jaimie Alexander, Cindi Pochatek
DESIGNERS › John Jaeckel, Cindi Pochatek, Karyn Kozo, Jim Hanika
ILLUSTRATOR/PHOTOGRAPHER › Stewart Shining
CLIENT › Hush Puppies
PAPER STOCK › Clark Graphics

DESIGN FIRM › Tycoon Graphics
ART DIRECTOR › Tycoon Graphics
DESIGNER › Tycoon Graphics
PHOTOGRAPHER › Shoji Uchida
CLIENT › Abahouse International Co., Ltd.

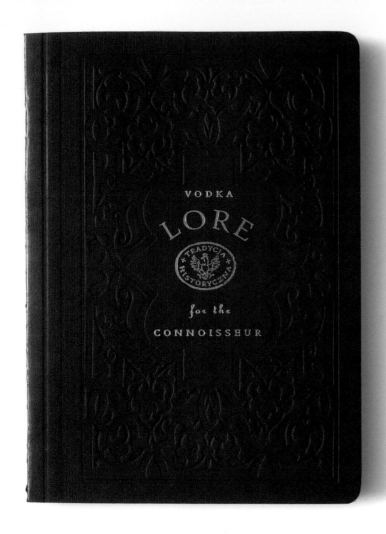

DESIGN FIRM > Clarity Coverdale Fury
ART DIRECTOR > Jac Coverdale
DESIGNER > Jac Coverdale
ILLUSTRATORS > Bill Cook, Peter Sjn, Kate Thomessen, Time Life Books
PHOTOGRAPHER > Raymond Meeks
COPYWRITER > Jerry Fury
CLIENT > Millennium Import Co.
TOOLS (SOFTWARE/PLATFORM) > Illustrator, QuarkXPress, Photoshop, Macintosh
PAPER STOCK > Cover: 130 lb. Curtis back linen; text: 80 lb. Cougar natural smooth
PRINTING PROCESS > Cover: foil stamped, two-colors; text: offset, six-colors, two sides

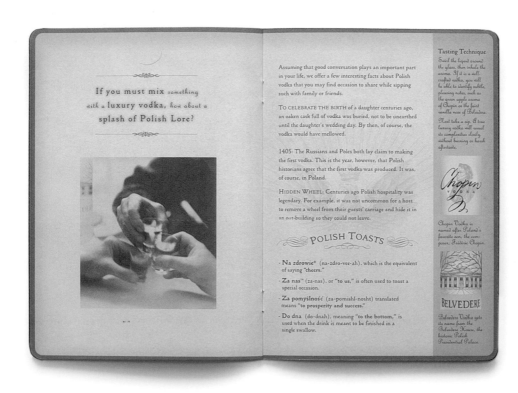

DESIGN FIRM › Sagmeister Inc.
ART DIRECTOR › Stefan Sagmeister
DESIGNER › Stefan Sagmeister
ILLUSTRATOR/PHOTOGRAPHER › Stefan Sagmeister
CLIENT › Anni Kuan Design
TOOLS (SOFTWARE/PLATFORM) › QuarkXPress
PAPER STOCK › Newsprint

six

six compelling reasons to

3 2 1

Six Red Marbles br
knowledge base to
eclectic background
in education, but a
and computer scier
A shared love of lea
intensely collaborat
rich, fresh, and inne

This depth of understanding extends to the
defing the vision behind a client's product

with your pedagogical n
specifications. Tools and p
shelf life of your solution. A
the difference between prove
latest flash in the pan.

In short,
consid

Anyone who thinks that an interacti
roject is going to be entirely smoo
ever developed one. While tim
ough and resources are seld
ates are usually carved in
y are fundamental piece
measure of anxiety.

A key facet o
feel better. T
production p
and schedule
than just deve
momentum w
logistical fact

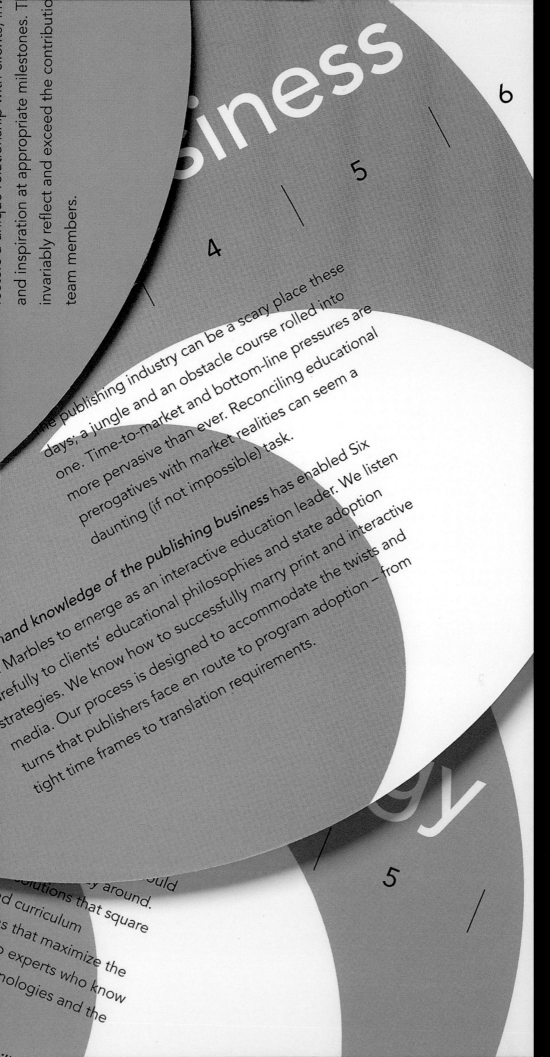

and inspiration at appropriate milestones. T
invariably reflect and exceed the contributio
team members.

6

5

4

...me publishing industry can be a scary place these
days; a jungle and an obstacle course rolled into
one. Time-to-market and bottom-line pressures are
more pervasive than ever. Reconciling educational
prerogatives with market realities can seem a
daunting (if not impossible) task.

...nd knowledge of the publishing business has enabled Six
...Marbles to emerge as an interactive education leader. We listen
...arefully to clients' educational philosophies and state adoption
...strategies. We know how to successfully marry print and interactive
media. Our process is designed to accommodate the twists and
turns that publishers face en route to program adoption – from
tight time frames to translation requirements.

5

...olutions that square
...y around.
...d curriculum
...s that maximize the
...e experts who know
...nologies and the

DESIGN FIRM › Julia Tam Design
ART DIRECTOR › Julia Tam
DESIGNER › Julia Tam
ILLUSTRATORS/PHOTOGRAPHERS › Miscellaneous
COPYWRITER › Dennis Moore
CLIENT › Samjorie Houlihan Lokey
TOOLS (SOFTWARE/PLATFORM) › QuarkXPress, Illustrator
PRINTING PROCESS › Five-color, varnish

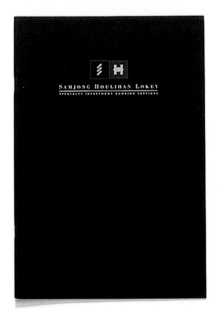

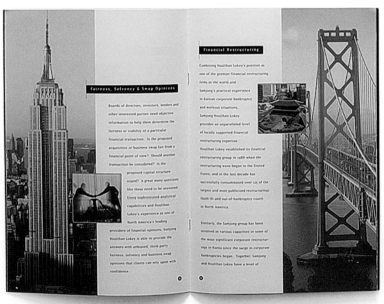

DESIGN FIRM › Austin Design
ART DIRECTOR › Wendy Austin
DESIGNER › Wendy Austin
PHOTOGRAPHER › Mark Ferri
CLIENT › Mark Ferri Photography
TOOLS (SOFTWARE/PLATFORM) › Envelopes, Cromatica, Absinthe, Yellow
PAPER STOCK/PRINTING PROCESS › Four-color Heidleberg Press, 100 lb. Potlatch vintage velvet gloss with a dull varnish
PRINTER › Arlington Lithograph

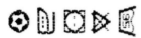

NAAM: THEO VERGEER · CLUB: DE GRAAFSCHAP

NAAM: JOHANNA KRUIZE · CLUB: PSV

Giving business more power
TO OPERATE IN TODAY'S WORLD

Business

law+science®

KELLER AND HECKMAN HELPED THE NATIONAL RURAL TELECOMMUNICATIONS COOPERATIVE NEGOTIATE THE LAUNCH OF THE FIRST SUCCESSFUL DIRECT BROADCAST SATELLITE VENTURE IN THE COUNTRY. THEY NOW HAVE MORE THAN ONE MILLION SUBSCRIBERS.

Businesses must respond to public concern, as well as laws and regulations. They care about the effect of their products, processes, and practices on their immediate community…and the entire planet. They care about the safety of their products and how they are made, handled, and transported. And, they care about the well-being of their most important resource—their people—all while safeguarding corporate profitability.

Keller and Heckman brings combined legal, regulatory, and scientific experience to these many issues. In the U.S., our people have helped develop and advise on the food safety, environmental, telecommunications, transportation, workplace safety, and labor policies that govern business activity. In the European Union, our Brussels office is expert at guiding clients through regulatory hurdles. As a result, wherever clients operate, we can help them cost-effectively meet their responsibilities, balancing the demands of society with the needs of stockholders. If our clients face legal action, Keller and Heckman can mobilize in-house scientific and technical staff to help frame legal positions based on solid data.

IN A WORLD THAT CAN BE HAZARDOUS FOR MANY INDUSTRIES, WE MAKE IT SAFER TO DO BUSINESS.

DESIGN FIRM > Jill Tanenbaum Graphic Design & Adv.
ART DIRECTORS > Jill Tanenbaum, Leah Germann
DESIGNERS > Jill Tanenbaum, Leah Germann
COPYWRITER > Jean Podgorsky
CLIENT > Keller & Heckman LLP
TOOLS (SOFTWARE/PLATFORM) > QuarkXPress, Illustrator, Macintosh

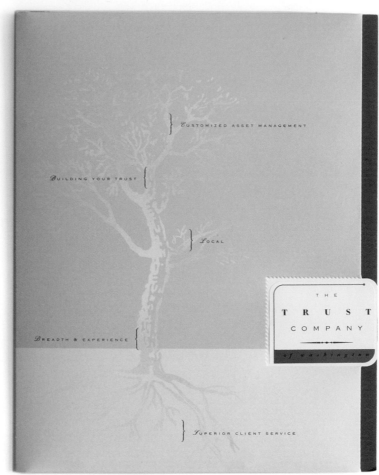

DESIGN FIRM › David Lemley Design
DESIGNERS › David Lemley, Emma Wilson
ILLUSTRATOR/PHOTOGRAPHER › Modified Clip Art
COPYWRITER › Jeff Fraga
CLIENT › The Trust Company of Washington
TOOLS (SOFTWARE/PLATFORM) › Freehand, QuarkXPress, Photoshop, Macintosh OS
PAPER STOCK › Neenah class columns bright white recycled
PRINTING PROCESS › Three PMS double-bumped, offset litho deboss and hand applied tip-in

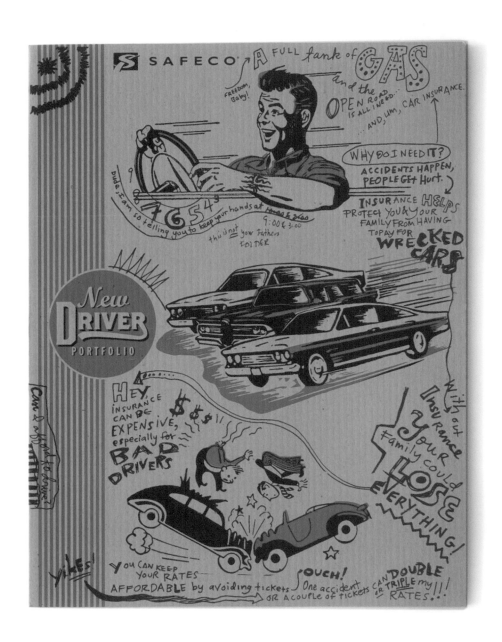

DESIGN FIRM > David Lemley Design
DESIGNERS > David Lemley, Emma Wilson
ILLUSTRATORS/PHOTOGRAPHERS > Modified Clip Art and DLD
COPYWRITER > Derek Dujardin
CLIENT > Safeco
TOOLS (SOFTWARE/PLATFORM) > Freehand, QuarkXPress, Photoshop, Macintosh OS
PAPER STOCK > Neenah classic columns, marigold, indigo
PRINTING PROCESS > Three PMS, offset lithography

DESIGN FIRM > David Lemley Design
DESIGNERS > David Lemley, Emma Wilson
ILLUSTRATORS > David Lemley, Emma Wilson
COPYWRITERS > Rogers & Hammerstein, David Lemley, Emma Wilson
CLIENT > Overlake Press
TOOLS (SOFTWARE/PLATFORM) > Freehand, QuarkXPress, Photoshop, Macintosh OS
PAPER STOCK > French Parchtone
PRINTING PROCESS > Four match colors, offset lithography

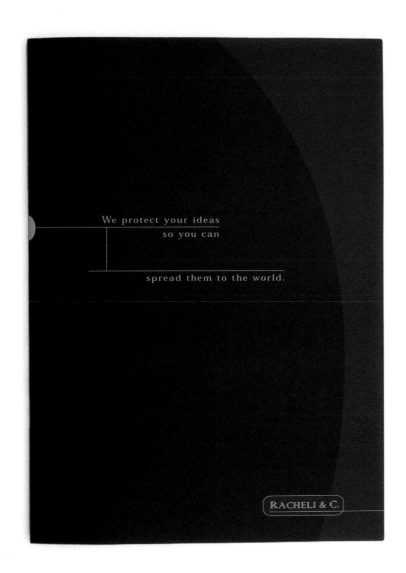

We protect your ideas
so you can

spread them to the world.

RACHELI & C.

DESIGN FIRM › Inox Design, Milan
ART DIRECTOR › Claudio Gavazzi
DESIGNER › Claudio Gavazzi
COPYWRITER › Michela Sartorio
CLIENT › Racheli & Co.
TOOLS (SOFTWARE/PLATFORM) › QuarkXPress
PAPER STOCK › Zanders T2000, two coated papers
PRINTING PROCESS › Three-color offset, opaque varnish, U.V. gloss varnish

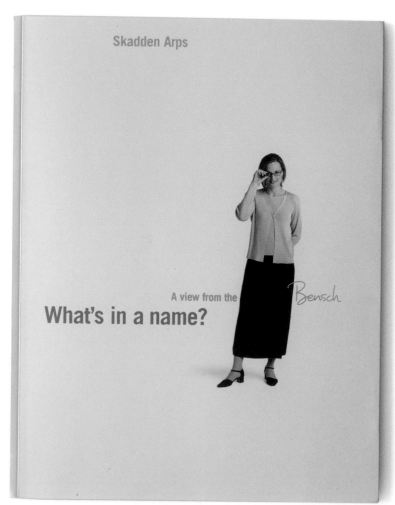

DESIGN FIRM › Carbone Smolan Agency
ART DIRECTOR › Justin Peters
DESIGNER › Ken Carbone
PHOTOGRAPHER › Erica Freudenstein
COPYWRITERS › Skadden Arps, Frank Oswald
CLIENT › Skadden Arps
TOOLS (SOFTWARE/PLATFORM) › QuarkXPress 4.1
PAPER STOCK/PRINTING PROCESS › Cover, stock 90 lb. Utopia premium silk white;
text: 115 lb. Utopia premium silk white

Dawn M. Pacifico
Associate, Labor
New York Office

Rutgers University
School of Law, Newark
(J.D. 1998)
Managing Editor, Rutgers
Law Review

Montclair State College
(B.S. 1995)

Law Clerk, Honorable
Richard Newman, New
Jersey Superior Court,
Appellate Division

Dawn of a new age

It's a wired world. And Skadden, Arps is at the heart of it all. Our clients include a wide range of tech-savvy firms—from large multinationals implementing Internet strategies to emerging high-tech companies in a number of sectors. Our newest offices in Palo Alto and Northern Virginia make us one of the few law firms with a presence in all major U.S. technology markets, including New York, Boston and LA.

17

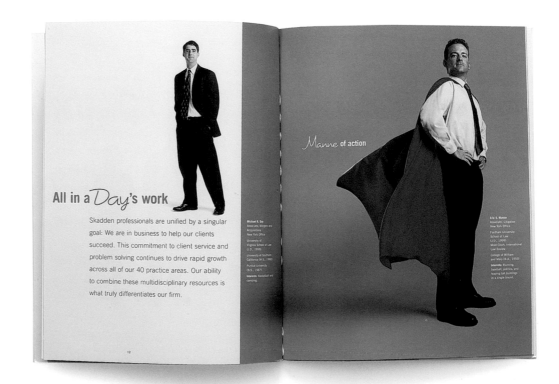

All in a *Day's* work

Skadden professionals are unified by a singular goal: We are in business to help our clients succeed. This commitment to client service and problem solving continues to drive rapid growth across all of our 40 practice areas. Our ability to combine these multidisciplinary resources is what truly differentiates our firm.

Michael R. Day
Associate, Mergers and
Acquisitions
New York Office

University of
Virginia School of Law
(J.D. 1998)

University of Southern
California (M.S., 1980)

Purdue University
(B.S., 1977)
Interests: Basketball and
camping.

12

Manne of action

Eric S. Manne
Associate, Litigation
New York Office

Fordham University
School of Law
(J.D. 1999)
Moot Court, International
Law Review

College of William
and Mary (B.A., 1993)

Interests: Running,
baseball, politics, and
leaping tall buildings
in a single bound.

It takes more than just a great idea to start a company. It takes the right market focus, a good management team, and an extensive network of resources and industry contacts to build a successful enterprise. Communications Ventures is uniquely qualified to assist early-stage companies develop into future industry leaders.

Communications Ventures is the preeminent venture capital firm in the communications industry. The firm invests exclusively in early-stage communications and networking companies, and has an unsurpassed investment record in the industry.

We put things together.

Communications Ventures is ideally positioned to invest in the companies that will emerge as the new leaders of the industry. The principals, CLIFFORD H. HIGGERSON, ROLAND A. VAN DER MEER, and DAVID P. HELFRICH have been actively involved in most major advances in the communications industry over the past two decades. As investors, directors, and managers they have played key roles in the formation of many of the industry's leading companies, including but not limited to Advanced Fibre Communications, America Online, Ascend, Broadcom, Ciena, Copper Mountain, Digital Microwave, Interom, itCi, Newbridge, Octel, PairGain, Paradyne, Tellabs, and 3Com.

Communications Ventures is not like every other venture capital firm. From any one, entrepreneurs only deal with the principals of the firm. By focusing on one industry, the firm is able not only to keep ahead of the trends but to anticipate them. The partners know the technology, the market dynamics, and the industry, which gives their portfolio companies the edge over the competition.

At Communications Ventures, few investment opportunities go unseen. One must have a broad view of the industry as well as specific technical expertise to be able to make investment decisions in such a complex area as communications.

Our underlying investment philosophy at Communications Ventures is to focus 120% on communications and networking. As a result, we are able to leverage our expertise, better identify exceptional opportunities, and help our portfolio companies achieve long-term success. The partners are willing to "think outside of the box" and look for opportunities that are unique and have great market potential. Once a business plan is received, we are able to react quickly and intuitively.

We see what others don't.

The partners have the ability to foresee key trends and market opportunities. This in turn has produced some of the most successful start-up companies and the highest returns of any venture firm that invests in the communications industry.

DESIGN FIRM › Gee + Chung Design
ART DIRECTOR › Earl Gee
DESIGNERS › Earl Gee, Fani Chung
PHOTOGRAPHER › Scott Peterson
COPYWRITERS › Kathleen Jensby, Roland Van der Meer
CLIENT › Communications Ventures
TOOLS (SOFTWARE/PLATFORM) › QuarkXPress, Adobe Illustrator, Photoshop
PAPER STOCK › Strathmore Writing bright white wove 110 lb. cover, Potlatch McCoy matte 100 lb. text
PRINTING PROCESS › Offset lithography foil stamping, blind embossing

DESIGN FIRM > Pisarkiewicz Mazur & Co. Inc.
ART DIRECTOR > Mary F. Pisarkiewicz
DESIGNER > Linda Farrer
CLIENT > KLS
TOOLS (SOFTWARE/PLATFORM) > QuarkXPress, Adobe Photoshop
PAPER STOCK > Curtis retrieve black cover, Ikono dull satin text,
Chartham steel blue (fly sheets)

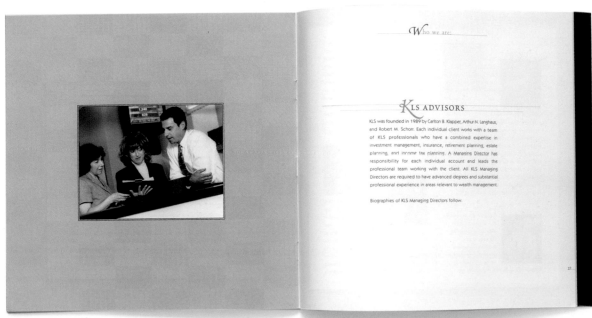

The Plaza Pavilion

4949 Wornall Road

Kansas City, Missouri

913-345-9300

The Plaza Pavilion

DESIGN FIRM › Tracy Design Communications, Inc.
ART DIRECTOR › Jan Tracy
DESIGNER › Anthony Magliano
ILLUSTRATORS/PHOTOGRAPHERS › Miscellaneous
COPYWRITER › Robin Zaplin
CLIENT › Bickford & Co.
TOOLS (SOFTWARE/PLATFORM) › QuarkXPress, Photoshop

DESIGN FIRM > IE Design
ART DIRECTOR > Marcie Carson
DESIGNER > Marcie Carson
CLIENT > Kern & Wooley LLP
TOOLS (SOFTWARE/PLATFORM) > Macintosh, Illustrator, Photoshop, QuarkXPress
PAPER STOCK/PRINTING PROCESS > Cover: Havana Structeras-Perla; text: Gilbert Oxford Cream
PRINTING PROCESS > Cover: two-color PMJS

DESIGN FIRM ❯ ie design, Los Angeles
CREATIVE DIRECTOR ❯ Marcie Carson
DESIGNER ❯ Marcie Carson
CLIENT ❯ Good Gracious Events

A boy named Devin had a box of dreams.
It was larger inside than out, it seemed,
for he pulled out a new dream every day,
he dreamed the dream, then tucked it away.
The dreams stayed nice and safe inside,
and no one could take them away if they tried.

DESIGN FIRM › Oden Marketing and Design
CREATIVE DIRECTOR › Bret Terwilleger
DESIGNER › Liz Fonville
ILLUSTRATOR › Bill Berry
COPYWRITERS › Liz Fonville, Sheperd Simmons
CLIENT › Boys and Girls Clubs of Greater Memphis

SOLUTIONS

OSBORN
MALEDON

www.osbornmaledon.com

DESIGN FIRM > After Hours Creative
ART DIRECTOR > After Hours Creative
DESIGNER > After Hours Creative
COPYWRITER > After Hours Creative
CLIENT > Osborn Maledon
TOOLS (SOFTWARE/PLATFORM) > Macintosh G4, Illustrator

COMPLEX

The best lawyers solve complicated problems in ways their clients can understand. • Osborn Maledon attorneys have the judgment, knowledge and experience to bring clarity to complex situations. You receive no-nonsense solutions to difficult business issues, from challenging litigation to mergers, acquisitions and public offerings. We know what it takes to get business done. And what it takes to help you achieve your goals. If everything were simple, your choice of a law firm wouldn't matter. When things get complicated, Osborn Maledon offers a clear solution.

CREATIVE

By moving just one glass, arrange the
top row to look like the bottom row.

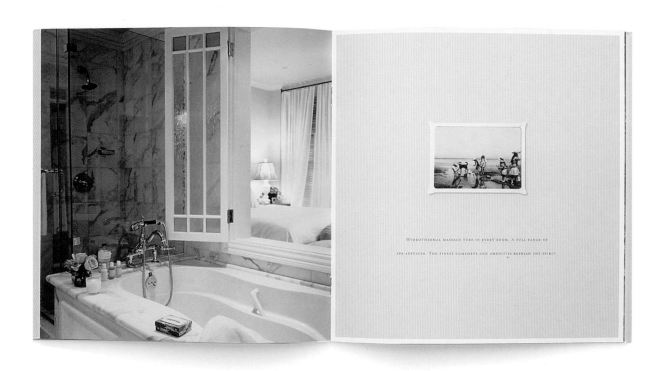

HYDROTHERMAL MASSAGE TUBS IN EVERY ROOM. A FULL RANGE OF

SPA SERVICES. THE FINEST COMFORTS AND AMENITIES REFRESH THE SPIRIT.

DESIGN FIRM > Arias Associates
ART DIRECTORS > Mauricio Arias, Maral Sarkis
DESIGNERS > Mauricio Arias, Maral Sarkis
COPYWRITER > Dawn Mortensen
CLIENT > Hotel Casa Del Mar
TOOLS (SOFTWARE/PLATFORM) > QuarkXPress, Photoshop, Illustrator
PAPER STOCK > Mohawk superfine and McCoy silk
PRINTING PROCESS > Lithography, embossing and letterpress

REGATTA
seaside residences

DESIGN FIRM > Arias Associates
ART DIRECTORS > Mauricio Arias, Maral Sarkis, Steve Mortensen, Stephanie Yee
DESIGNERS > Mauricio Arias, Maral Sarkis, Steve Mortensen, Stephanie Yee
ILLUSTRATOR/PHOTOGRAPHER > Fred Licht
COPYWRITER > Words by Design
CLIENT > Crescent Heights
TOOLS (SOFTWARE/PLATFORM) > QuarkXPress, Photoshop, Illustrator
PAPER STOCK > Starwhite Vicksburg
PRINTING PROCESS > Lithography, letterpress

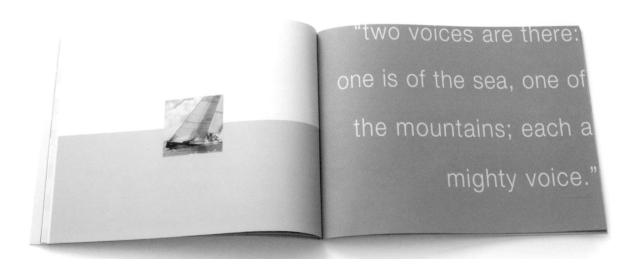

"two voices are there:
one is of the sea, one of
the mountains; each a
mighty voice."

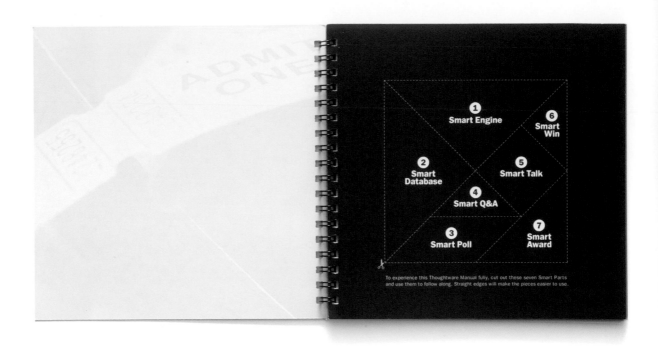

Anatomy of a *SmartSpiff*

When your Thoughtware calls for a *SmartSpiff* certificate, entry ticket or game piece, you can choose from many distinct constructions, shapes, sizes and materials. Design your *SmartSpiff* to adhere to your packaging with security features, or seal it in food barrier wrap for insertion with your product, or include a multi-fold brochure in your construction, or die cut a shape relating to your campaign's theme— virtually *anything* is possible.

The most cost-efficient construction is a two-ply, dry-seal rectangular format that peels apart and yields four copy panels. At right is an example shown at actual size.

10

DESIGN FIRM > Aspen Interactive
ART DIRECTOR > Ken Weightman
DESIGNER > Ken Weightman
CLIENT > Phoneworks
TOOLS (SOFTWARE/PLATFORM) > QuarkXPress, Adobe Photoshop, Macintosh
PAPER STOCK/PRINTING PROCESS > Four-color process and one match color

DESIGN FIRM › McMonigle & Associates
ART DIRECTOR › Jamie McConigle
DESIGNER › John Edwards
ILLUSTRATOR/PHOTOGRAPHER › Jamie McMonigle
COPYWRITER › Katrin Seher
CLIENT › Wescorp Investment Services
PAPER STOCK › Classic Crest

DESIGN FIRM > AXIS Communications
ART DIRECTOR > Craig Byers
DESIGNER > Craig Byers
ILLUSTRATOR/PHOTOGRAPHER > Thomas Arledge
CLIENT > Thomas Arledge
TOOLS (SOFTWARE/PLATFORM) > QuarkXPress, Macintosh
PAPER STOCK > Donside Gleneagle 100 lb. gloss, Proterra Kraft antique
PRINTING PROCESS > Four-color process

DESIGN FIRM › Sayles Graphic Design
ART DIRECTOR › John Sayles
DESIGNER › John Sayles
PHOTOGRAPHERS › David Crosby, Tony Smith
ILLUSTRATOR › John Sayles
COPYWRITER › Wendy Lyons
CLIENT › Greenville South Carolina Convention & Visitors Bureau
TOOLS (SOFTWARE/PLATFORM) › QuarkXPress, Macintosh
PRINTING PROCESS › Offset printed, includes tipped-on samples

perfect aim

perfect fit

DESIGN FIRM › Sibley Peteet Design
ART DIRECTOR › Donna Aldridge
DESIGNER › Donna Aldridge
ILLUSTRATOR › Brandon Kirk
COPYWRITER › Don Sibley
CLIENT › Williamson Printing Company
TOOLS (SOFTWARE/PLATFORM) › QuarkXPress, Macintosh
PAPER STOCK › Strobe

WE'RE BECOMING MORE CUSTOMER FOCUSED UP AND DOWN THE LINE.

The big picture. An assembly line worker in an auto plant is more than step number 12 in an eleven-step process. He understands that his job is directly tied to the work that comes before him and what will follow. At BNSF, we're embracing that same attitude toward our customers' businesses. We're learning the ins and outs of your business right down the line to understand the unique transportation needs of each of our business partners.

Creative thinking. Creative solutions. Meeting customer challenges has made us solution-prone. Sometimes solutions develop from the partnership. Sometimes the ground is the solution. In 1992, American Honda wanted to move imports faster than its midsize rivals did to deliver them through the Parsons Canal. BNSF created a "landbridge" which sliced the transit time in half. Recognizing a good thing when they saw it, Mercedes-Benz, Volkswagen and Nissan have begun using our landbridge options to market.

Faster to market. In recent years, sport utility vehicles (SUVs) have climbed to the top of the charts. To help supply keep pace with demand, we worked with our automotive customers to increase the "Autoway" which represents faster than one step SUV from their lanes. Autoway can provide 40 percent more capacity than traditional trailers. And because this is intermodal, the cars provide better ride quality at higher train speeds.

Autoway, BNSF's customer-driven highcapacity, is just another reason why two out of every three new cars and trucks sold in North America hit the rails before they hit the road.

Of the 4,685 parts on this car, which is the most important?

Mine.

WE'RE NOT JUST DELIVERING GOODS, WE'RE DELIVERING SOLUTIONS.

Flexible shipping for inflexible schedules. One size does not fit all when it comes to shipping. Just ask "the tightest ship in the shipping business." United Parcel Service, our largest customer, relies on a partner in guaranteed, on-time delivery. We help them line up to run with a high-speed network designed specifically to meet the right destination at it times in UPS hubs across the country. During the peak season between Thanksgiving and Christmas, BNSF especially ships over 82 million packages for UPS. Ours one. It is that kind of premium intermodal service that helped us set the industry record for the longest stretch of perfect service with UPS.

Innovative solutions for cool customers. Maybe you can wait for the next train, but your ice cream can't? That's why temperature-sensitive products like fruits, vegetables and frozen foods have traditionally traveled on refrigerated trucks. Not anymore. BNSF's Ice Cold Express gives customers fast, reliable, temperature-controlled transportation complete with real-time satellite tracking. How do customers describe the Ice Cold Express? Cool.

Linking the nation's largest retail chain. From the nation's largest retailer can't carry everything. That's why they come to us. For Wal-Mart, innovators at BNSF created a supply chain that linked every link. Working directly with the retail giant, we designed a coordinated intermodal system that manages freight through their entire transportation chain. We're the only U.S. railroad to have a direct intermodal alliance with a retail company. It happened because both Wal-Mart and BNSF knew there had to be a better way. Together, we found it.

There's always a cold front moving between Southern California and Chicago with BNSF's Ice Cold Express.

IN MY BUSINESS TIME IS MONEY. IF YOU'RE MAKING EXCUSES YOU'RE NOT MAKING MONEY.

DESIGN FIRM > Witherspoon Advertising
ART DIRECTOR > Alan Comtois
DESIGNER > Alan Comtois
COPYWRITER > Carol Glover
CLIENT > Burlington Northern Railroad
TOOLS (SOFTWARE/PLATFORM) > QuarkXPress, Photoshop, Macintosh
PAPER STOCK > Signature

DESIGN FIRM > Peterson & Co.
ART DIRECTOR > Nhan T. Pham
DESIGNER > Nhan T. Pham
ILLUSTRATORS/PHOTOGRAPHERS > Various
COPYWRITER > In-house
CLIENT > Meeting Professionals International
TOOLS (SOFTWARE/PLATFORM) > Quark 4.0, Illustrator 8.0, Photoshop 5.0
PAPER STOCK > Tierra 110 lb. Starwhite velum cover plus mac flat form

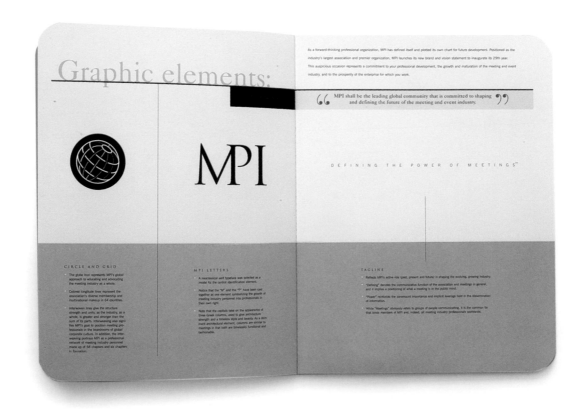

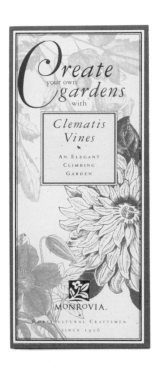

DESIGN FIRM > Erbe Design
ART DIRECTOR > Maureen Erbe
DESIGNER > Maureen Erbe
ILLUSTRATOR > Allison Starcher
COPYWRITER > Maureen Gilmer
CLIENT > Monrovia
TOOLS (SOFTWARE/PLATFORM) > QuarkXPress
PRINTING PROCESS > Lithography

Two Thousand Pounds

Two Thousand Pounds of Lead

Two Thousand Reasons to Keep on Trying

DESIGN FIRM > RBMM
ART DIRECTOR > Kenny Garrison
DESIGNER > Jim Jacobs
ILLUSTRATOR/PHOTOGRAPHER > Pete Lacker
COPYWRITER > Jim Jacobs
CLIENT > Williamson Printing Corp.
TOOLS (SOFTWARE/PLATFORM) > QuarkXPress, Photoshop

six compelling reasons to work with

sixredmarbles

| 1 | 2 | 3 | 4 | 5 | 6

DESIGN FIRM > Stoltze Design
ART DIRECTOR > Clifford Stoltze
DESIGNERS > Stacy Day, Brandon Blangger, Cynthia Patten
CLIENT > Six Red Marbles

DESIGN FIRM **>** Summa Comunicació
ART DIRECTORS **>** Wladimir Marnich, Griselda Marti
DESIGNERS **>** Wladimir Marnich, Griselda Marti
ILLUSTRATOR/PHOTOGRAPHER **>** Jose Luis Merino
COPYWRITER **>** Summa Comunicació - Espacio Pyme
CLIENT **>** Espacio Pyme
TOOLS (SOFTWARE/PLATFORM) **>** Freehand
PAPER STOCK **>** Uncoated stock
PRINTING PROCESS **>** Offset

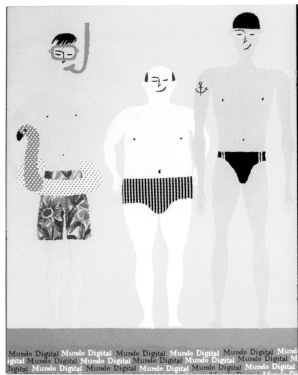

A quién nos dirigimos. www.espaciopyme.com se ha creado para satisfacer las necesidades de un mercado dinámico formado por numerosas pymes de multiples **sectores**. Nuestro proyecto se dirige a todas aquellas empresas con predisposición al cambio y con voluntad de apostar por las nuevas tecnologías e Internet como medio de futuro. Por ello, ofrecemos asesoramiento y soluciones a empresas con diferentes

niveles

de conocimiento y experiencia en la Red: tanto a empresas debutantes como a aquéllas que tienen un grado de familiarización medio con las nuevas tecnologías. A todas ellas, Espacio Pyme les ofrece su **ayuda** en este proceso de adaptación.

Qué es Espacio Pyme. Un espacio virtual donde las pequeñas y medianas empresas podrán aprovecharse de las ventajas que el **mundo digital** supone para su negocio y encontrar, en una única web, un acceso directo a una extensa oferta de **soluciones.** www.espaciopyme.com ha sido creado con un objetivo muy claro:

acercar

las nuevas tecnologías a las pymes y poner a su disposición información, servicios y herramientas que las ayuden a ser más competitivas. Confiar en Espacio Pyme significa obtener un conjunto de **ventajas** gracias a una amplia oferta de servicios de alta calidad y a bajo coste, ventajas que, hasta el día de hoy, estaban reservadas exclusivamente a las grandes empresas.

Nuevas Tecnologías

WHY JACK CHARLTON IS NOT A BIG BELIEVER IN FRICTION

Reels.

STREAMWORKS

BAG IT, PACK IT, FLOAT IT OR JUST PLAIN USE IT

Gear

DESIGN FIRM › Hornall Anderson Design Works, Inc.
ART DIRECTOR › Jack Anderson
DESIGNERS › Jack Anderson, Belinda Bowling, Andrew Smith, Ed Lee
ILLUSTRATOR › Jack Unruh
COPYWRITERS › Various
CLIENT › Streamworks
TOOLS (SOFTWARE/PLATFORM) › QuarkXPress, Photoshop
PAPER STOCK › French Speckletone Kraft cover, natural text

DESIGN FIRM > Lee Reedy Creative
ART DIRECTOR > Lee Reedy
DESIGNER > Lee Reedy
ILLUSTRATOR/PHOTOGRAPHER > Stock
COPYWRITER > Suzy Patterson
CLIENT > Travel Connections
TOOLS (SOFTWARE/PLATFORM) > QuarkXPress
PAPER STOCK > Chipboard
PRINTING PROCESS > Two-color

DESIGN FIRM > DBD International, Ltd
ART DIRECTOR > David Brier
DESIGNER > David Brier
ILLUSTRATOR > David Brier
PHOTOGRAPHER > Fredrik Broden
COPYWRITER > Steve Ferry
CLIENT > Rubin Baum
TOOLS (SOFTWARE/PLATFORM) > Macintosh, QuarkXPress, Illustrator
PAPER STOCK > Potlatch McCoy
PRINTING PROCESS > Four-color

THE NEW STANDARD It's not about which platform or manufacturer. It's about you, greater control, and limitless compatibility, across the hall — or across the globe. You're entering the first platform-compatible world of technology. Be wary of "computer resellers" who try to pitch other alternatives. As a pro-active technology supplier, Digital Minds is now offering the future and the way work will be done, rather than merely providing tomorrow's soon-to-be-extinct rave. Imagine: conflict-free workflow... platform to platform. It's almost as unbelievable as world peace.

DESIGN FIRM > DBD International, Ltd.
ART DIRECTOR > David Brier
DESIGNER > David Brier
ILLUSTRATOR > David Brier
PHOTOGRAPHER > Jake Armour
COPYWRITER > David Brier
CLIENT > Digital Minds
TOOLS (SOFTWARE/PLATFORM) > Macintosh, QuarkXPress, Illustrator
PRINTING PROCESS > Color process, vintage gloss and delustered polymer laminate

the

in

ies

very

rare, and

Japanese

Family

Health

Program

University of Michigan

Health System

DESIGN FIRM › Wagner Design
ART DIRECTORS › Laura Herold, Kazuko Sacks
DESIGNER › Jill Wagner
COPYWRITER › Toni Voss
CLIENT › University of Michigan, Department of Family Medicine, Japanese Family Health Program
TOOLS (SOFTWARE/PLATFORM) › QuarkXPress, Photoshop
PAPER STOCK › Folder: Neenah Environment Sedona red, 80 lb. cover; Insert: Warren Lustre dull cream, 80 lb. cover
PRINTING PROCESS › Inserts: four-color; folder: one spot color plus foil stamp

DESIGN FIRM > Didier Saco Design
ART DIRECTOR > Didier Saco
DESIGNER > Laurent Dumte
ILLUSTRATOR/PHOTOGRAPHER > Cendrine Ronsard
CLIENT > Festival D'Art Lyrique Aiten Provence
PAPER STOCK > Verge 110 grammes

DESIGN FIRM > Giovanni Design Associates
ART DIRECTORS > John Frontino, Edward Maichin
DESIGNERS > John Frontino, Edward Maichin
ILLUSTRATOR/PHOTOGRAPHER > Stock
COPYWRITER > Advertising Council
CLIENT > Advertising Council
TOOLS (SOFTWARE/PLATFORM) > QuarkXPress, Photoshop

DESIGN FIRM > O & J Design Inc.
ART DIRECTORS > Barbara Olejniczak, Lia Camera Mariscal
DESIGNERS > Barbara Olejniczak, Lia Camera Mariscal
ILLUSTRATOR/PHOTOGRAPHER > David Radler
COPYWRITERS > Kalen Blinn, Mimi Koren
CLIENT > Isabella Geriatric Center
TOOLS (SOFTWARE/PLATFORM) > QuarkXpress
PAPER STOCK/PRINTING PROCESS > Cover: three-color; interior: two-color

DESIGN FIRM > Zappata Diseñadores S.C.
ART DIRECTOR > Ibo Angulo
DESIGNER > Ibo Angulo
CLIENT > Nuevo Mundo University
TOOLS (SOFTWARE/PLATFORM) > Photoshop, Freehand, Macintosh
PRINTING PROCESS > Offset, couche

EVERYONE
NEEDS A
HERO

The Doctors' Company

DESIGN FIRM > Oh Boy, A Design Company
ART DIRECTOR > David Salanitro
DESIGNER > Ryan Mahar
PHOTOGRAPHER > Scott Goldsmith
COPYWRITERS > Susan Wilkinson, Dana Cooper-The Doctors' Company
CLIENT > The Doctors' Company
PAPER STOCK > Superfine, ultra white smooth

NEONATAL NURSE

11:50
Female. Name: Sarah Elizabeth
Garner. Weight 6 lbs. 9 oz.
Born: 1/5/00 at 07:16.
Father: Nicholas Garner.
Mother: Andrea Garner.

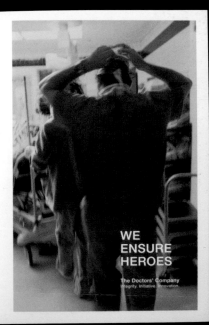

WE
ENSURE
HEROES

The Doctors' Company
Integrity. Initiative. Innovation.

DESIGN FIRM > Shamlian Advertising
ART DIRECTOR > Brian DiRienzi
DESIGNER > Brian DiRienzi
CLIENT > ESF Summer Camps
TOOLS (SOFTWARE/PLATFORM) > Photoshop, Macintosh
PAPER STOCK/PRINTING PROCESS > 4/4

DESIGN FIRM > Gee + Chung Design
ART DIRECTOR > Earl Gee
DESIGNERS > Earl Gee, Fani Chung
PHOTOGRAPHER > Steve Jost
COPYWRITERS > Stephanie Lasenza, Gary Hawk
CLIENT > Alliance Healthcare Foundation
TOOLS (SOFTWARE/PLATFORM) > QuarkXPress, Adobe Illustrator, Photoshop
PAPER STOCK > Potlatch Karma natural 100 lb. text, French Paper Co., Speckletone Madero beach white 70 lb. text
PRINTING PROCESS > Offset lithography, blind embossing

DESIGN FIRM > Parsons Promotion Design
ART DIRECTORS > Evelyn Kim, Meg Callery
DESIGNERS > Evelyn Kim, Meg Callery
ILLUSTRATOR/PHOTOGRAPHER > Marty Heitner
COPYWRITERS > Carole Schaffer, Hilary Howard
CLIENT > Parsons Undergraduate Catalog
TOOLS (SOFTWARE/PLATFORM) > QuarkXPress, Photoshop, Illustrator

STUDENTS

For the first time, **they like going to class.**

They can't believe how well they fit in. They are amazed at their **new abilities.**

They can now **visualize their future.**

DESIGN FIRM > The Art Institute of Seattle
ART DIRECTOR > Scott Engelhardt
DESIGNER > Scott Engelhardt
PHOTOGRAPHER > Zee Wendell
COPYWRITER > Susan Goschie
CLIENT > The Art Institute of Seattle
TOOLS (SOFTWARE/PLATFORM) > Macintosh, QuarkXPress
PAPER STOCK > Cougar opaque
PRINTING PROCESS > Sheet fed

THE CENTER FOR COSMETIC
AND LASER SURGERY

American Society
of Plastic Surgeons

American Society
for Aesthetic Plastic Surgery

Board Certified by the
American Board of Plastic Surgery

AAAASF-The American Association
for Accreditation
of Ambulatory Surgery Facilities

DESIGN FIRM › Griffin Design
ART DIRECTOR › Tracy Griffin Sleeter
DESIGNER › Tracy Griffin Sleeter
ILLUSTRATOR › Rick Kessinger
PHOTOGRAPHER › Stock photography
COPYWRITER › Cindy Lorimor
CLIENT › Center for Cosmetic & Laser Surgery
TOOLS (SOFTWARE/PLATFORM) › Macintosh
PRINTING PROCESS › Offset with aqueous coating, embossed foil stamp,
Bloomington Offset Process, Inc.

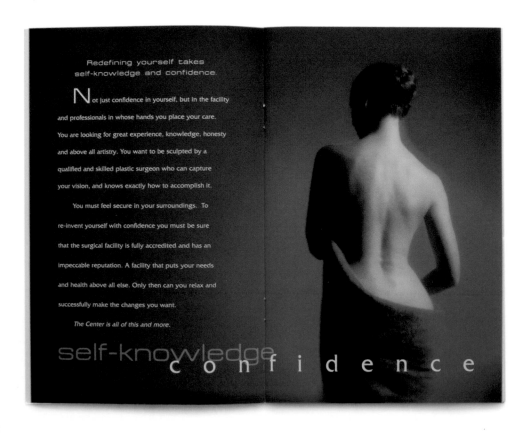

Redefining yourself takes
self-knowledge and confidence.

Not just confidence in yourself, but in the facility and professionals in whose hands you place your care. You are looking for great experience, knowledge, honesty and above all artistry. You want to be sculpted by a qualified and skilled plastic surgeon who can capture your vision, and knows exactly how to accomplish it.

You must feel secure in your surroundings. To re-invent yourself with confidence you must be sure that the surgical facility is fully accredited and has an impeccable reputation. A facility that puts your needs and health above all else. Only then can you relax and successfully make the changes you want.

The Center is all of this and more.

self-knowledge
confidence

DESIGN FIRM ❯ Oh Boy, A Design Company
ART DIRECTOR ❯ David Salanitro
DESIGNER ❯ Alice Chang
PHOTOGRAPHER ❯ Tony Stone Images
COPYWRITER ❯ Son Rant
CLIENT ❯ Thap!
PAPER STOCK ❯ Caress eggshell 80 lb.
PRINTING PROCESS ❯ Offset, sheet fed

!augh

Laugh and the whole world laughs with you. Laughing relaxes muscles, increases heart rate, improves the oxygenation of blood and releases positive mood-enhancing endorphins which all lead to longer, healthier and happier lives.

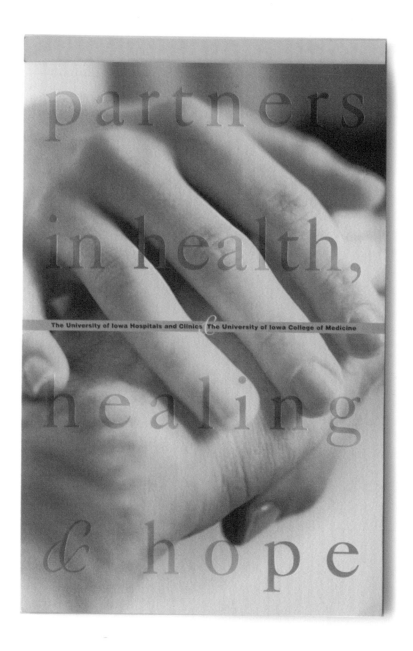

partners in health, healing & hope

The University of Iowa Hospitals and Clinics & The University of Iowa College of Medicine

DESIGN FIRM > University of Iowa Foundation
ART DIRECTOR > Theresa Black
DESIGNER > Theresa Black
ILLUSTRATORS/PHOTOGRAPHERS > Jon Van Allen, Diane Hill, Reggie Morrow
COPYWRITER > Claudia Reinhardt
CLIENT > VI Foundation
TOOLS (SOFTWARE/PLATFORM) > Pagemaker, Photoshop, Macintosh
PAPER STOCK > Gilbert Voice
PRINTING PROCESS > Three PMS colors

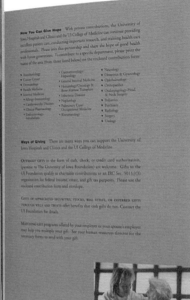

DESIGN FIRM › SamataMason
ART DIRECTOR › Greg Samata
DESIGNER › Kevin Kureger
PHOTOGRAPHERS › Sandro, Martha Brock
CLIENT › WITS (Working in the Schools)
TOOLS (SOFTWARE/PLATFORM) › QuarkXPress, Macintosh
PAPER STOCK › French Speckletone Chipboard,
Appleton Utopia two matt and Springhill Incentive
PRINTING PROCESS › Offset printing, sheet fed

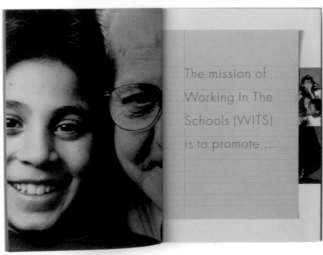

Being adopted

is like being a puzzle with

a missing piece.

DESIGN FIRM > AXIS Communications
ART DIRECTOR > Craig Byers
DESIGNER > Tamara Dowd
ILLUSTRATOR > Becky Heavner
PHOTOGRAPHER > Robert Burke
COPYWRITER > Kathy Mitchell, Tamara Dowd
CLIENT > The Center for Adoption Support and Education
TOOLS (SOFTWARE/PLATFORM) > QuarkXPress, Macintosh
PRINTING PROCESS > 4-color

american academy of microbiology

The American Academy of Microbiology is the honorific leadership group within the American Society for Microbiology (ASM), the world's oldest and largest life science organization. The mission of the American Academy of Microbiology is to recognize scientists for outstanding contributions to microbiology and provide microbiological expertise in the service of science and the public.

The Academy serves as a resource to governmental agencies, industry, ASM, and the larger scientific and lay communities by convening colloquia to address critical issues in microbiology. The Academy brings together a group of scientific experts for several days of structured, directed deliberations, resulting in an analytical, practical, objective report that is widely disseminated.

The Academy, through its sponsorship of the American College of Microbiology, certifies outstanding microbiologists in clinical and industrial specialties and accredits postdoctoral training programs in clinical and public health microbiology and immunology. The Academy also manages a stellar awards program, recognizing achievement and potential in all areas of microbiology.

DESIGN FIRM > Pensaré Design Group, Ltd.
ART DIRECTOR > Mary Ellen Vehlow
DESIGNER > Kundia D. Wood
ILLUSTRATOR/PHOTOGRAPHER > Photodisc Stock Photography
COPYWRITERS > Carol Colgan, American Academy of Microbiology

Rymdteknik

Space Science Related to Satellites

20 POÄNG – HALVFART

Utbildningens mål

Vem vänder sig linjen till

Linjens struktur och innehåll

Ytterligare information

20

ingenjörs VETENSKAP

Ingenjörsvetenskap

Rymdte...

20 POÄNG

Kursmoment

22

23

Fortbildningslinjer   för

yrkesverksamma
civilingenjörer
och
arkitekter

2000

CHALMERS

DESIGN FIRM > Göthberg + Co. Design
ART DIRECTOR > Bengt Göthberg
DESIGNER > Bengt Göthberg
ILLUSTRATOR > Bengt Göthberg
PHOTOGRAPHER > Jens Karlsson
CLIENT > Chalmers Tekniskr Hogsköla
PAPER STOCK > Woodfree uncoated

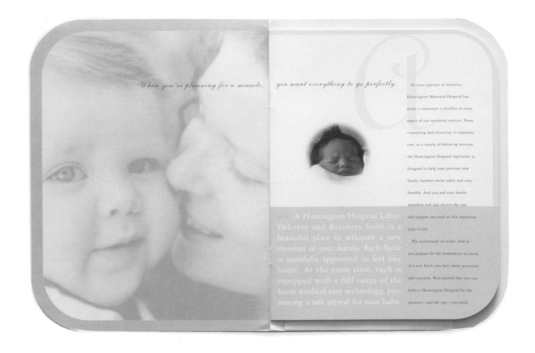

DESIGN FIRM › Erbe Design
ART DIRECTOR › Maureen Erbe
DESIGNER › Maureen Erbe
ILLUSTRATOR/PHOTOGRAPHER › Scott Streble
COPYWRITER › Victoria Thurlough
CLIENT › Huntington Hospital
TOOLS (SOFTWARE/PLATFORM) › QuarkXPress
PRINTING PROCESS › Lithography

DESIGN FIRM › Gardner Design
ART DIRECTOR › Brian Miller
DESIGNER › Travis Brown
CLIENT › Kansas Joint Replacement Institute
TOOLS (SOFTWARE/PLATFORM) › Freehand, Photoshop
PRINTING PROCESS › Four-color

DESIGN FIRM > Danette Angerer
ART DIRECTOR > Danette Angerer
DESIGNER > Danette Angerer
ILLUSTRATORS/PHOTOGRAPHERS > Mike Schlotterback, Mark Trade, Rod Bradley, Michael Ask, Jeff Schmatt
COPYWRITER > Elinor Day
CLIENT > Brucemore
TOOLS (SOFTWARE/PLATFORM) > Pagemaker, Macintosh
PAPER STOCK > Dust cover: Environment Desert Storm. Cover: Environment Sedona Red.
Flysheet: U.V./Ultra II sepia interior. Interior stock: Sterling satin.
PRINTING PROCESS > Four-color process, PMS 876 metallic and spot dull varnish
PRINTER > Garner Printing, Des Moines, IA

Different Drugs
ALCOHOL

Other names:

Ale, beer, booze, drink, plonk, sherbet, spirits, wine.

Under the influence...

Off your head/face, pissed, sozzled, drunk, stoned, tiddly, tipsy.

Background information:

Alcoholic drinks are produced by the process of fermenting fruit, grain or vegetables to produce an intoxicating drink which may vary in alcohol content. Distillation of the fermented product produces spirits with a higher concentration of alcohol.

How it is taken:

Alcohol is usually swallowed as a drink.

Effects and risks:

Alcohol is a depressant drug which slows down the Central Nervous System.

Small amounts: remove inhibitions, relaxes.
Large amounts: loss of co-ordination, slurred speech, double vision, nausea and/or vomiting,
Very large amounts: unconsciousness, possible heart attack, coma or death.

Alcohol is rapidly absorbed into the blood stream. The first effects are almost immediate and vary greatly depending on how much is taken, how quickly it is drunk, body weight, age and sex, *(alcohol affects women more than it affects men)*, and whether other drugs have been taken or food eaten.

A tolerance to alcohol and possibly dependence may develop with sustained use. Sudden withdrawal from severe alcohol dependence can be life threatening. Physical effects of prolonged heavy use include an increased risk of liver cirrhosis, stomach ulcers, cancers of the mouth, stomach and throat, heart disease, pancreatitis, brain damage and destruction of nerve cells.

Excessive regular drinking commonly aggravates family, personal and financial problems. *(see **Drug Problems** for more detailed information).*

Legal status:

Alcohol may only be sold under licence to a person over the age of 18 but may be drunk by anyone (see **Drugs and the Law** for more detailed information).

Did you know?

Regular consumption in excess of the daily benchmarks of 3-4 units a day for men and 2-3 units a day for women may cause significant health risks.

———— 1 UNIT IS EQUAL TO ————

Half a pint of ordinary beer, lager or cider	Quarter of a pint of strong beer, lager or cider	One small glass of wine, sherry or port	One 25ml measure of spirit or liqueur

a parent's guide to drugs

DESIGN FIRM > Advertising International Limited
ART DIRECTOR > Robin Ovenden
DESIGNER > Robin Ovenden
COPYWRITER > Trevor Alborough

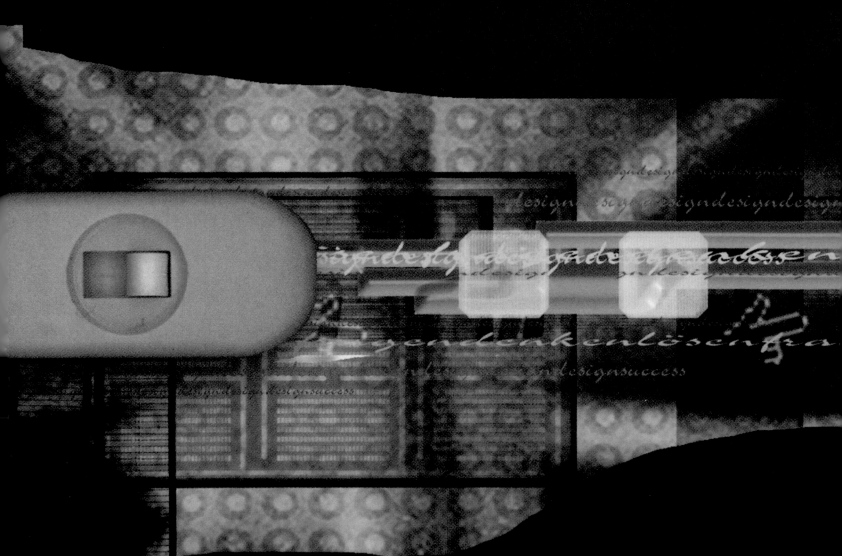

SELF-PROMOTIONALTIONAL
BROCHURES

DESIGN FIRM › Emery Vincent Design
ART DIRECTOR › Garry Emery
DESIGNER › Emery Vincent Design
CLIENT › Emery Vincent Design
TOOLS (SOFTWARE/PLATFORM) › QuarkXPress, Illustrator, Photoshop

Sakata 1995

The Ian Potter Museum of Art, The University of Melbourne 1998

Melbourne Exhibition Centre 1996

<24/25

I have never seen the practice as part of the mainstream, nor as part of the avant garde, but as occupying some sort of curious middle ground, with a keen interest in new media and the digital future. There is no special focus on two-, three- or four-dimensional design, simply a general interest in each. Similarly there is equal commitment to large, small and middle-sized projects, as well as an interest in both the cultural and the commercial – although to every commercial project we endeavour to bring a cultural dimension. Our practice happily occupies its own territory (Garry Emery)

04 The work

Fox Furniture 1995

Emery Vincent Design specialises in three principal areas of design: individual and brand identity and corporate communications, print and electronic media, and environmental graphic design including exhibitions. Clients are from the private and public sectors, including corporations, institutions, manufacturers, professional service and cultural organisations. Projects range in scale from a page to an entire city. Approximately half the work is print and electronic-based and the other half is environmental graphic design.

Among the many public projects by the practice are the rejuvenation of the Australia Post identity, the new identity and signage for the National Gallery of Victoria, and signage programs for the Australian Embassies in Beijing and Tokyo, Brisbane and Melbourne International Airport terminals, Cathay Pacific international headquarters in Hong Kong, Kuala Lumpur City Centre, Melbourne Exhibition Centre, Melbourne Museum, Parliament House of Australia, The Ian Potter Museum of Art Melbourne, Powerhouse Museum Sydney, State Library of Victoria, Sydney Opera House, Sydney 2000 Olympics site, the design of the Built on Gold exhibition in the Old Treasury Museum Melbourne, as well as Australian currency and postage stamps.

Aside from commercial projects, the practice conducts a number of in-house projects to test certain ideas and extend the practice of graphic design. Objects such as Vessel – Millennial/Perennial, and a studio table, Otto, are examples of these exploratory exercises.

My background is that of a traditional typographer, influenced by modernism and calligraphy (in particular the calligraphy of Edward Johnson) (Garry Emery)

Built on Gold Exhibition, Old Treasury Museum Melbourne 1998

<22/23

DESIGN FIRM > Magma
ART DIRECTORS > Lars Harmsen, Axel Brinkman, Uli Weiss
DESIGNERS > Lars Harmsen, Axel Brinkman, Uli Weiss
CLIENT > Magma

DESIGN FIRM › Graif Design
ART DIRECTOR › Matt Graif
DESIGNER › Matt Graif
CLIENT › Seven Course Design
TOOLS (SOFTWARE/PLATFORM) › Illustrator 9.0
PAPER STOCK › Neenah Paper Co.
PRINTING PROCESS › Offset printing

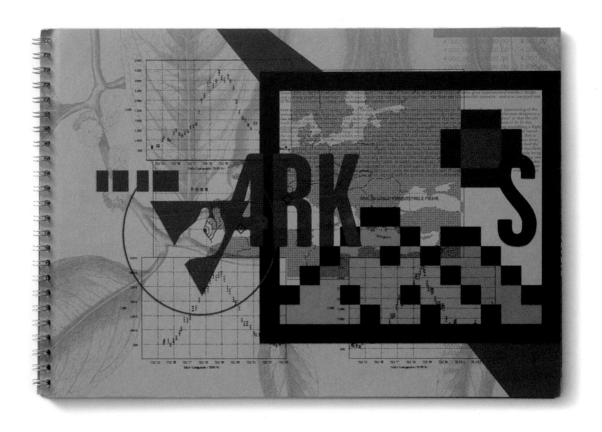

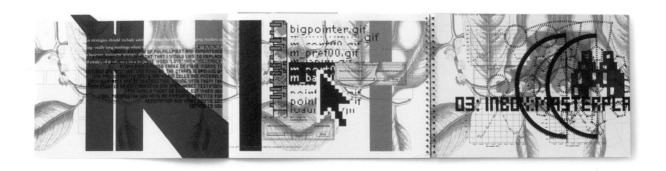

DESIGN FIRM › Fork Unstable Media GMBH
ART DIRECTOR › David Linderman
DESIGNER › David Linderman
COPYWRITER › David Linderman
CLIENT › Fork Unstable Media
TOOLS (SOFTWARE/PLATFORM) › Freehand 8.0, Photoshop 5.5,
Capture v 4.0, Macintosh platform
PAPER STOCK › Gmund "Havanna," Munken "Munken Pur"
PRINTING PROCESS › Three-color, U.V. glaze

DESIGN FIRM > Pepe Gimeno - Proyecto Gráfico
ART DIRECTOR > Pepe Gimeno
DESIGNERS > Suso Pérez, José P. Gill
CLIENT > Pepe Gimeno - Proyecto Gráfico
TOOLS (SOFTWARE/PLATFORM) > Freehand 8.0, Photoshop 5.
PRINTING PROCESS > Offset

DESIGN FIRM › Kan & Lau Design Consultants
ART DIRECTOR › Freeman Lau Siu Hong
DESIGNER › Freeman Lau Siu Hong
CLIENT › Kan & Lau Design Consultants
TOOLS (SOFTWARE/PLATFORM) › Freehand 8.0, Photoshop 5.0
PAPER STOCK › 157 Gulliver

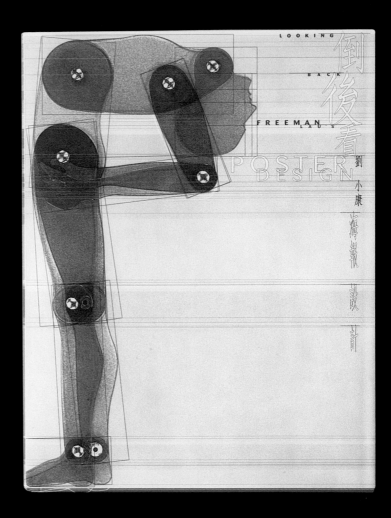

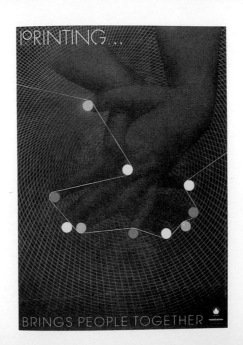

DESIGN FIRM > Libby Perszyk Kathman
ART DIRECTOR > Matt Baughan
DESIGNER > Matt Baughan
ILLUSTRATORS/PHOTOGRAPHERS > Brad Holland, Jeff Kauck, Dane Heithaus, Greg Kuchik
COPYWRITER > John Recker
CLIENT > Libby Perszyk Kathman
TOOLS (SOFTWARE/PLATFORM) > Illustrator, Photoshop, Macintosh
PAPER STOCK > 100 lb. centura gloss cover and text
PRINTING PROCESS > Offset

DESIGN FIRM › IE Design

ART DIRECTOR › Marcie Carson

DESIGNER › Marcie Carson

ILLUSTRATOR/PHOTOGRAPHER › Kevin Merrill

COPYWRITER › Marcie Carson

CLIENT › IE Design

TOOLS (SOFTWARE/PLATFORM) › Macintosh, Illustrator, Photoshop, QuarkXPress

PAPER STOCK › Gilbert esse, Gilelcar Oxford

PRINTING PROCESS › Four-color

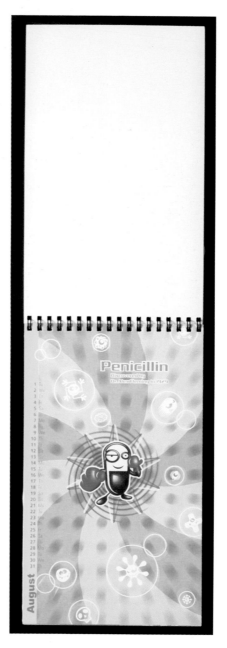

DESIGN FIRM > ARTiculation Group/Wilco Design
ART DIRECTORS > Joseph Chan, Wilson Lam
DESIGNERS > Joseph Chan, Wilson Lam, Helena Ng, Karin Fukuzawa
PHOTOGRAPHERS > Joseph Chan, Steven Chan, see spot run and various stock
COPYWRITERS > David Savoie, Pramila David
CLIENT > ARTiculation Group
TOOLS (SOFTWARE/PLATFORM) > Photoshop
PAPER STOCK > Strathmore

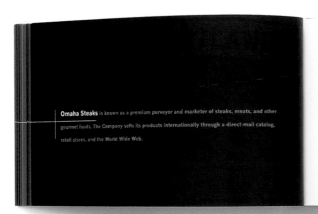

Omaha Steaks is known as a premium purveyor and marketer of steaks, meats, and other gourmet foods. The Company sells its products internationally through a direct-mail catalog, retail stores, and the World Wide Web.

DESIGN FIRM > Fitch
ART DIRECTOR > Mark Uskavich
DESIGNER > Mark Uskavich
ILLUSTRATOR/PHOTOGRAPHER > Mark Uskavich
CLIENT > Fitch
PRINTING PROCESS > Baesman Printing

foco

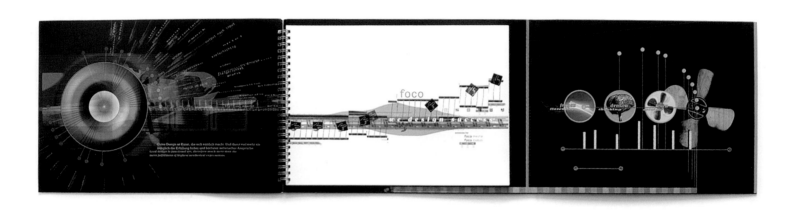

DESIGN FIRM > Foco Media gmbh & cte
ART DIRECTOR > Steffen Janus
DESIGNER > Steffen Janus
CLIENT > Foco Media gmbh & cte

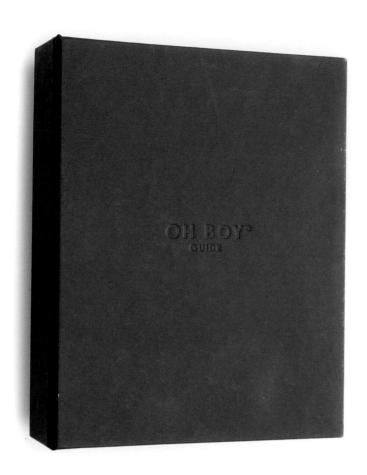

DESIGN FIRM > Oh Boy, A Design Company
ART DIRECTOR > David Salanitro
DESIGNERS > Hunter Wimmer, Ted Bluey
PHOTOGRAPHER > Hunter Wimmer
COPYWRITERS > David Salanitro, Hunter Wimmer
CLIENT > Oh Boy, A Design Company
PAPER STOCK > Mohawk 65 lb. superfine, ultrawhite
PRINTING PROCESS > Offset, sheet fed

DESIGN FIRM > Witherspoon Advertising
ART DIRECTOR > Rishi Seth
DESIGNER > Rishi Seth
COPYWRITER > Rishi Seth
CLIENT > Witherspoon Advertising
TOOLS (SOFTWARE/PLATFORM) > QuarkXPress, Illustrator, Macintosh
PAPER STOCK > Starwhite Vicksburg
PRINTING PROCESS > Offset

Iomega: Zip, Clik!, and Jaz drives
Repositioning to create the future

As computer users become more sophisticated, they become more demanding – wanting affordable data storage systems with capacity to capture, share, organize, and protect all their business and personal 'stuff'.

The Iomega Corporation, an established leader in manufacturing removable data storage products, sought to move beyond their traditional business to business and professional market sectors. They briefed Fitch to reposition their brand and change the way consumers and the marketplace think about data storage products.

Research with both techno savvy and casual users showed that while portable data storage was something consumers needed and wanted, they felt alienated by marketing aimed at computer experts. The new brand positioning, packaging, and communications used straightforward language rather than technical jargon, and product names were kept short, fun, and memorable. Even the Iomega identity was given a lower case 'i' to make it friendlier.

Our research also uncovered several product voids in the market which led to the development of the original 100MB Zip drive. Subsequent product additions have included the Jaz, Ditto, Clik! and Zip 250 drives.

These products have enabled Iomega to deliver technology that not only addresses real user needs, but has also given our client ownership of an entirely new category of the computer peripherals market. In March 1999 Iomega announced that it had shipped 25 million Zip drives and 150 million disks to date, and the company currently commands 87% of the removable data storage market. Zip has become a generic household name – the Hoover of data storage.

01 The Zip 250 offers two-and-a-half times the storage capacity of the original Zip drive.

02 Iomega packaging communicates product features and capabilities in easy-to-understand, non-technical language.

03 The Iomega Clik! enables simple, fast transfer of digital image files.

25 Million Zip drives shipped to date

iomega
zip 250
25 million
1

Consumers want useful, usable and desirable products – served by technology rather than driven by it

User Research
Consumer Research
Brand Strategy
Product Design
Engineering
Packaging
Graphic Design
Information Architecture
Information Design
User Interface Design
Naming
Video Graphics
Exhibition Design
Interactive Design
Programming

DESIGN FIRM > Fitch
ART DIRECTOR > Carol Dean
DESIGNER > Nick Richards
COPYWRITER > Jennifer Wood
CLIENT > Fitch

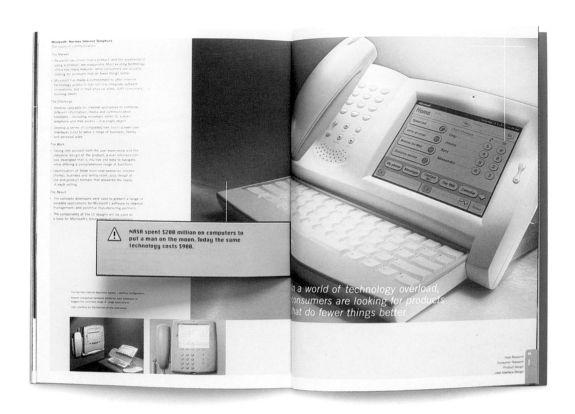

Microsoft: Hermes Internet Telephone
The future of communication

The Market
- Research has shown that a product, and the experience of using a product, are inseparable. Most existing technology offers too many features, while consumers are actually looking for products that do fewer things better.
- Microsoft has made a commitment to offer Internet technology products that not only integrate software innovations, but in their physical state, fulfil consumers' evolving needs.

The Challenge
- Develop concepts for Internet appliances to combine different information, media and communication functions – including vo-email, caller ID, e-mail, telephone and Web access – in a single object.
- Develop a series of completely new touch screen user interfaces (UIs) to serve a range of business, family and personal uses.

The Work
- Taking into account both the user experience and the industrial design of the product, a user interface (UI) was developed that is intuitive and easy to navigate while offering a comprehensive range of functions.
- Identification of three main user scenarios: kitchen (home), business and family room, plus design of UIs and product formats that answered the needs of each setting.

The Result
- The concepts developed were used to present a range of possible applications for Microsoft's software to internal management, and potential manufacturing partners.
- The components of the UI designs will be used as a base for Microsoft's future product development.

⚠ NASA spent $200 million on computers to put a man on the moon. Today the same technology costs $900.

The Hermes Internet Appliance system – desktop configuration.

Several conceptual hardware platforms were developed to suggest the unlimited range of usage applications.

User interface for the Hermes phone appliances.

In a world of technology overload, consumers are looking for products that do fewer things better

User Research
Consumer Research
Product Design
User Interface Design

DESIGN FIRM > Fitch
ART DIRECTOR > Vassoula Vasiliou
DESIGNER > Kian Kuan
CLIENT > Fitch

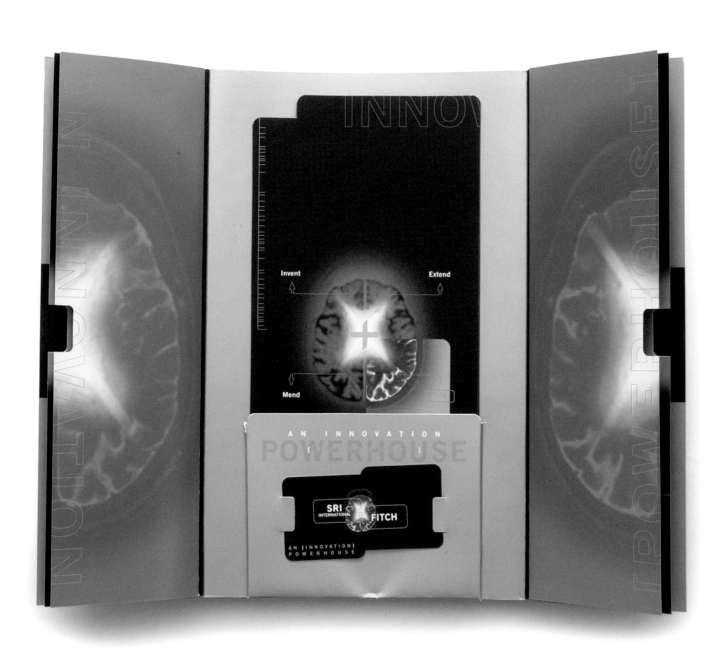

DESIGN FIRM › Louey/Rubino Design Group Inc.

ART DIRECTOR › Robert Louey

DESIGNERS › Robert Louey, Alex Chao, Anja Mueller

ILLUSTRATORS/PHOTOGRAPHERS › Eric Tucker, Jamey Stillings, Everard Williams Jr., Lise Metzger, Neal Brown, Ann Elliot Cutting, Hugh Kretschmer

COPYWRITER › Elisabeth Charney

CLIENT › Louey/Rubino Design Group

TOOLS (SOFTWARE/PLATFORM) › QuarkXPress, Macintosh

PAPER STOCK › Mead Signature dull, Gilbert Oxford

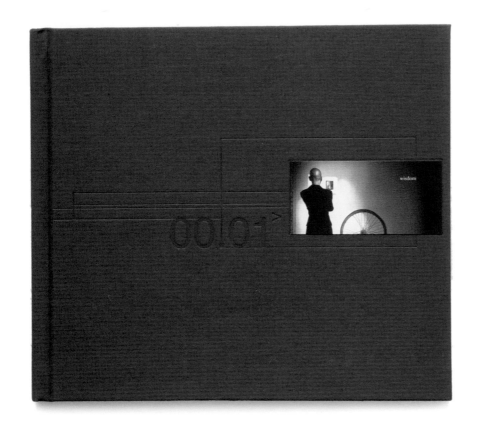

HANGE ORDERS
r. Michael Cohen

ome Directors have
ported a decline in
thusiasm from
embers who are looking
or something more than
he same old thing.'
a few cases, there
as been an overall
ecline in attendance
nd even drop-outs.
r. Cohen will draw
n his own
xperience to
xplore the likely
auses and offer
hange orders"
esigned to
reate a
ewarding, longer
sting, and more
uccessful
tudy club
xperience.

DESIGN FIRM › IT IS DESIGN Co.
ART DIRECTOR › Tomohior Itami
DESIGNER › Tomohior Itami
ILLUSTRATOR/PHOTOGRAPHER › Satoshi Hirose
CLIENT › TBS -J Britannica Co., Ltd.
TOOLS (SOFTWARE/PLATFORM) › Macos, Photoshop, Illustrator, QuarkXPress
PAPER STOCK/PRINTING PROCESS › Mr. B White

DESIGN FIRM › Hoffman Angelic Design
ART DIRECTOR › Andrea Hoffman
DESIGNER › Andrea Hoffman
ILLUSTRATOR › Ivan Angelic
CLIENT › The Seattle Study Club
TOOLS (SOFTWARE/PLATFORM) › Macintosh, Illustrator 8.0

DESIGN FIRM › Bolt

ART DIRECTORS › Jamey Boiter, Mark Thwaites, Deanna Mancuso

DESIGNERS › Jamey Boiter, Mark Thwaites, Deanna Mancuso

ILLUSTRATOR/PHOTOGRAPHER › Stephanie Chesson

COPYWRITERS › IDSA & Bolt

CLIENT › IDSA

TOOLS (SOFTWARE/PLATFORM) › Photoshop, Illustrator, QuarkXPress

PRINTING PROCESS › 4-color, spot metallic

AUX YEUX DU
TRÈS-HAUT, IL
N'EXISTE NI PLAINE
NI HAUTEUR.
TOUTE HAUTEUR EST
NIVELÉE, ET
NUL HOMME
N'EST PETIT ET
NUL HOMME N'EST
IMPOSANT *Les Mille et Une Nuits*

DESIGN FIRM > Future Brand, London
ART DIRECTOR > Wladimir Marnich
DESIGNER > Wladimir Marnich
ILLUSTRATOR/PHOTOGRAPHER > Magnum Photos
COPYWRITERS > L. Hertwig, R. Gautron, E. Steiner
CLIENT > Council of Europe
TOOLS (SOFTWARE/PLATFORM) > QuarkXPress
PAPER STOCK > Coated, silk finish
PRINTING PROCESS > Offset

CALEIDOSCÓPIO.
Ficha Artística e Técnica

Criação e Argumento
Teatro Bruto

Texto
Vânia Covas

Encenação
Ana Luena e Paulo Freixinho

Cenografia e Figurinos
Ana Luena

Desenho de Luz
José Álvaro

Vídeo
Paulo Américo

Banda Sonora
Quico

Apoio ao Movimento
Joana Providência

Apoio Vocal
Céu Ribeiro

Intérpretes
Carlos Peixoto
Marcello Porfecarreiro
Mário Santos
Miguel Cabral
Paulo Freixinho
Bruno

Canção de Bonitares
Letra: Vânia Covas/adaptação Quico
Voz: Rute Pimenta
Coros: Nuno Aragão

Spot Publicitário Espuma de Banho
Susana Menezes

Coordenação de Montagem de Som
Quico

Montagem e Operação de Som
Diaco Vasligaro

Montagem e Operação de Luz
José Álvaro

Operação de Vídeo
Paulo Américo

Adereços e apoio à montagem de cenografia
Cláudia Antunes

Concretização de Mesas e Cadeiras
André Lima

Costureira
Branca Vhan

Fotografia
Margarida Ribeiro

Design Gráfico
Artur Rebelo e Lisa Ramalho @ R2 Design

Assistência de Produção
Rute Miranda

Produção
Teatro Bruto

DESIGN FIRM > R2 Design
ART DIRECTORS > Lizá Defossez Ramalho, Artur Rebelo
DESIGNER > Lizá Defossez Ramalho, Artur Rebelo
ILLUSTRATORS/PHOTOGRAPHERS > Lizá Defossez Ramalho, Margarida Ribeiro
CLIENT > Teatro Bruto
TOOLS (SOFTWARE/PLATFORM) > Freehand, Photoshop
PAPER STOCK > Munken lynx
PRINTING PROCESS > Offset

DESIGN FIRM › Greteman Group
ART DIRECTORS › Sonia Greteman, James Strange
DESIGNERS › James Strange, Craig Tomson
COPYWRITERS › Deanna Harms, David Kamerer
CLIENT › Royal Caribbean
TOOLS (SOFTWARE/PLATFORM) › Freehand, Photoshop
PAPER STOCK/PRINTING PROCESS › Strathmore Elements smooth bright white

DESIGN FIRM › Trickett & Webb Ltd.
DESIGNERS › Lynn Trickett, Brian Webb, Katja Thielen
PHOTOGRAPHER › Adam Mitchinson
CLIENT › The London Institute
TOOLS (SOFTWARE/PLATFORM) › QuarkXPress
PAPER STOCK › Munken Lynx and Parilux
PRINTING PROCESS › Four-color lithography

DESIGN FIRM > Sayles Graphic Design
ART DIRECTOR > John Sayles
DESIGNER > John Sayles
ILLUSTRATOR > John Sayles
CLIENT > Pattee Enterprises
TOOLS (SOFTWARE/PLATFORM) > QuarkXPre
PRINTING PROCESS > Offset

DESIGNERS > Lanny Sommese, Pat Creyts

ILLUSTRATOR/PHOTOGRAPHER > Lanny Sommese

COPYWRITER > Rick Bryant

CLIENT > Central Pennsylvania Festival of the Arts

TOOLS (SOFTWARE/PLATFORM) > Macintosh, Adobe Illustrator, QuarkXPress

PAPER STOCK > Beckett concept vellum

PRINTING PROCESS > Offset

CALL FOR ENTRIES CENTRAL PENNSYLVANIA FESTIVAL OF THE ARTS 34TH SIDEWALK SALE AND EXHIBITION JULY 13-16

CALL FOR ENTRIES CENTRAL PENNSYLVANIA FESTIVAL OF THE ARTS CHILDREN AND YOUTH SIDEWALK SALE JULY 12

CALL FOR ENTRIES CENTRAL PENNSYLVANIA FESTIVAL OF THE ARTS CRAFTS NATIONAL 34 JURIED FINE CRAFT EXHIBITION JUNE 2-JULY 21

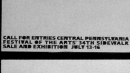

CALL FOR ENTRIES CENTRAL PENNSYLVANIA FESTIVAL OF THE ARTS' BANNER COMPETITION 2000 JULY 12-16

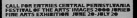

CALL FOR ENTRIES CENTRAL PENNSYLVANIA FESTIVAL OF THE ARTS' IMAGES 2000 JURIED FINE ARTS EXHIBITION JUNE 20-JULY 20

DESIGN FIRM > Dana Collins
ART DIRECTOR > Dana Collins
DESIGNER > Dana Collins
ILLUSTRATOR/PHOTOGRAPHER > Dana Collins
CLIENT > LA Weekly Theater Awards
TOOLS (SOFTWARE/PLATFORM) > Corel Draw, Photoshop, QuarkXPress

DESIGN FIRM > Inox Design, Milan
ART DIRECTORS > Alessandro Floridia, Mauro Pastore
DESIGNERS > Alessandro Floridia, Mauro Pastore
COPYWRITER > Elena Schiavi
CLIENT > MTV Networks
TOOLS (SOFTWARE/PLATFORM) > Freehand
PAPER STOCK/PRINTING PROCESS > Plexiglass, acetate, four-color offset printing, one-color (white) serigraphic

DESIGN FIRM › IE Design
ART DIRECTOR › Marcie Carson
DESIGNER › Marcie Carson
ILLUSTRATOR/PHOTOGRAPHER › Nadine Froger
COPYWRITERS › Liese Gardner, Susan Cuadrado
CLIENT › Extraordinary Events
TOOLS (SOFTWARE/PLATFORM) › Macintosh, Illustrator, Photoshop, QuarkXPress
PRINTING PROCESS › Four-color, lenticular tip-in

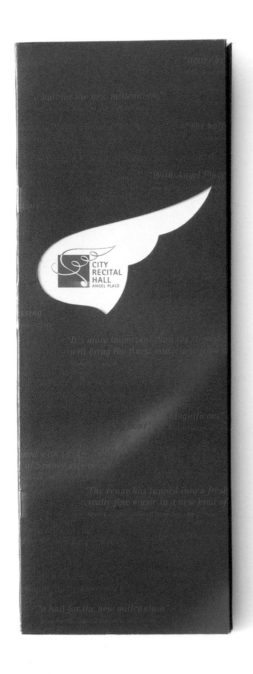

DESIGN FIRM > Spatchurst Design Associates
ART DIRECTOR > John Spatchurst
ILLUSTRATOR/PHOTOGRAPHER > John Spatachurst
CLIENT > City Recital Hall, Angel Place
TOOLS (SOFTWARE/PLATFORM) > Illustrator, Photoshop, QuarkXPress, Macintosh Platform
PRINTING PROCESS > Offset

DESIGN FIRM › Oh Boy, A Design Company
ART DIRECTOR › David Salanitro
DESIGNERS › Ryan Mahar, David Salanitro, Ted Bluey
ILLUSTRATORS/PHOTOGRAPHERS › Ryan Mahar, Hunter Wimmer, Photonica, The Stock Market, FPG International
COPYWRITER › Carol Baxter
CLIENT › Mercury Interactive
PAPER STOCK › 50 lb. Lynx
PRINTING PROCESS › Offset, sheet fed

DESIGN FIRM > AXIS Communications
ART DIRECTOR > Craig Byers
DESIGNER > Tamara Dowd
ILLUSTRATOR/PHOTOGRAPHER > Various
COPYWRITER > S.I.T.E.S. (Smithsonian Institution Traveling Exhibition Service)
CLIENT > S.I.T.E.S. (Smithsonian Institution Traveling Exhibition Service)
TOOLS (SOFTWARE/PLATFORM) > QuarkXPress, Macintosh
PAPER STOCK > Donside Consort Royal, osprey, silk tint, 100 lb text and cover
PRINTING PROCESS > Four-color, plus two PMS and varnish

DESIGN FIRM ❯ Lowercase, Inc.
ART DIRECTOR ❯ Tim Bruce
DESIGNER ❯ Tim Bruce
ILLUSTRATOR/PHOTOGRAPHER ❯ Tim Bruce
CLIENT ❯ Writers' Theatre Chicago
TOOLS (SOFTWARE/PLATFORM) ❯ QuarkXPress, Macintosh
PAPER STOCK ❯ Cougar

DESIGN FIRM › INOX Design, Milan
ART DIRECTORS › Claudio Gavazzi, Sabrina Elena
DESIGNERS › Claudio Gavazzi, Sabrina Elena
COPYWRITER › Michela Sartorio
CLIENT › MTV Networks
TOOLS (SOFTWARE/PLATFORM) › QuarkXPress, Photoshop
PAPER STOCK/PRINTING PROCESS › Opaque coated paper
PRINTING PROCESS › Four-color offset, gloss varnish

DESIGN FIRM ❯ LA Weekly
ART DIRECTOR ❯ Sheryl Scott
DESIGNER ❯ Sheryl Scott
CLIENT ❯ LA Weekly Music Awards
TOOLS (SOFTWARE/PLATFORM) ❯ QuarkXPress, Photoshop

ADVERTISING INTERNATIONAL LIMITED
7 Bath Street, St. Helier
Jersey, C.I. JE24ST
United Kingdom
Tel: 01534 730001
Fax: 01534 735412
E-mail: adagent@ilt.net

AFTER HOURS CREATIVE
5444 E. Washington, Suite 3
Phoenix, Arizona 85034
Tel: 602-275-5200
Fax: 602-275-5700

ALTERNATIVES
875 6th Avenue, 26th Floor
New York, New York 10001
Tel: 212-239-0600
Fax: 212-239-1625
E-mail: julie@alternativesdesign.com

ARIAS ASSOCIATES
502 Waverley Street
Palo Alto, California 94301
Tel: 650-321-8138
Fax: 650-321-9250
E-mail: maral@ariasassociates.com

ARTICULATION GROUP/WILCO DESIGN
33 Bloor St. East, Suite 1205
Toronto, Ontario M4W 3T4
Canada
Tel: 416-922-7999
Fax: 416-922-1683
E-mail: joseph@articulationgroup.com

ASPEN INTERACTIVE
7036 Park Drive
New Port Richey, Florida 34652
Tel: 727-849-8166
E-mail: kweightman@aspenmg.com

AUSTIN DESIGN
161 Paradise Road
Swampscott, Massachusetts 01907
Tel: 781-593-4360
Fax: 781-593-5640
E-mail: wendyaustin@mindspring.com

AXIS COMMUNICATIONS
729 15th Street NW, Suite 900
Washington, DC 20005
Tel: 202-347-0060
Fax: 202-347-5331

BASE ART CO.
112 Oakland Park Ave.
Columbus, Ohio 43214
Tel: 614-268-3061
Fax: 614-268-3062
E-mail: base@ee.net

BBK STUDIO
5242 Plainfield Avenue NE
Grand Rapids, Michigan 49525
Tel: 616-447-1460
Fax: 616-447-1461
E-mail: yang@bbkstudio.com

BLOCH + COULTER DESIGN GROUP
2440 S. Sedelveda Blvd. #152
Los Angeles, California 90064
Tel: 310-445-6550
Fax: 310-445-6555
E-mail: victoria@blochcoulter.com

BOLT
1415 S. Church Street
Charlotte, North Carolina 28227
Tel: 704- 372-2658
Fax: 704-372-2655
E-mail: thwaites@mindspring.com

THE BONSEY DESIGN PARTNERSHIP PTE LTD
179 River Valley Road
05-01 River Valley Building
Singapore 179033
Tel: 65 339 0428
Fax: 65 339 0418
E-mail: postmaster@bonsey.com.sg

BURROWS
The Burrows Building
5 Rayleigh Road
Shenfield, Essex CM13 1AB
United Kingdom
Tel: 44 1277 246666
Fax: 44 1277 246777
E-mail: roy-hearne@burrows.impiric.com

CARBONE SMOLAN AGENCY
22 West 19th Street
New York, New York 10011
Tel: 212-807-0011
Fax: 212-807-0870
E-mail: leslie@carbonesmolan.com

CLARITY COVERDALE FURY
120 South 6th Street, Suite 1300
Minneapolis, Minnesota 55402
Tel: 612-359-4304
Fax: 612-359-4392
E-mail: treadwell@ccf-ideas.com

COUNTRY COMPANIES DESIGN SERVICES
1711 GE Road
Blooming, Illinois 61701
Tel: 309-821-2758
E-mail: tracy.sleeter@countrycompanies.com

COX DESIGN
5196 Hummingbird Road
Pleasanton, California 94566
Tel: 925-484-2711
E-mail: rcox@sjmercury.com

CREATIVE CONSPIRACY INC.
862 Main Ave., Suite 205
Durango, Colorado 81301
Tel: 970-247-2262
Fax: 970-247-1386
E-mail: nhannum@creativeconspiracy.com

CRITT + GRAHAM + ASSOCIATES
2970 Clairmont Road, Suite 850
Atlanta, Georgia 30329
Tel: 404-320-1737
Fax: 404-320-1920
E-mail: erin@crittgraham.com

CROSS COLOURS INK
8 Eastwood Road
Dunkeld West 2196 Johannesburg
South Africa
Tel: 27 11 442 2080
Fax: 27 11 442 2086
E-mail: cross@iafrica.com

DAMION HICKMAN DESIGN
22975 Caminito Olivia
Laguna Hills, California 92653
Tel: 949-261-2857
Fax: 949-261-5966
E-mail: DHD2YN@primenet.com

DAVID LEMLEY DESIGN
8 Boston Street, #11
Seattle, Washington 98109
Tel: 206-285-6900
Fax: 206-285-6906
E-mail: david@lemleydesign.com

DBD INTERNATIONAL, LTD.
406 Technology Drive West
Menomonie, Wisconsin 54751
Tel: 715-235-9040
Fax: 715-235-9323
E-mail: dbrier@dbdintl.com

DIDIER SACO DESIGN
10 Rue Des Jeuneurs
Paris 75002 France
Tel: 01 40 26 9696
Fax: 01 40 96 9596

DINNICK & HOWELLS
2943 Markham Street
Toronto, Ontario M6J 296
Canada
Tel: 416-921-5754
Fax: 416-921-0719
E-mail: jonathan@dinnickhowells.com

DOUGLAS JOSEPH PARTNERS
11999 San Vincente Blvd., Suite 201
Los Angeles, California 90049
Tel: 310-440-3100
Fax: 310-440-3103
E-mail: slambert@djpartners.com

**EDELMAN PUBIC RELATIONS WORLDWIDE
(ENKI)**
636 Broadway, Suite 707
New York, New York 10012
Tel: 212-505-3543
Fax: 212-505-0846
E-mail: lana@enkiny.com

EMERY VINCENT DESIGN
80 Market Street
Southbank, Victoria 3006
Australia
Tel: 61 3 9699 3822
Fax: 61 3 9690 7371
E-mail: alison.orr@evd.com.au

ERBE DESIGN
1500 Oxley Street
South Pasadena, California 91030
Tel: 626-799-9892
Fax: 626-799-0906
E-mail: studio@erbedesign.com

FITCH
10350 Olentangy River Road
Worthington, Ohio 43085
Tel: 614-885-3453
Fax: 614-885-4289
E-mail: christina_cooney@fitch.com

FOCO MEDIA GMBH & CTE
Spitzwegstr 6
Munich 81373 Germany
Tel: 49 89 7463240
Fax: 49 89 74632424
E-mail: casar@focomedia.de

FORK UNSTABLE MEDIA GMBH
Juliusstrasse 25
Hamburg 22769 Germany
Tel: 49 40 432948 14
Fax: 49 40 432948 11
E-mail: svenja@fork.de

FOSSIL
2280 N. Greenville Avenue
Richardson, Texas 75082
Tel: 972-699-2125
Fax: 972-699-2071
E-mail: steven2@fossil.com

FUTURE BRAND, LONDON
Roger de Lluria 124
Parcelona 08037 Spain
Tel: 34 93 459 1477
Fax: 34 93 459 1010
E-mail: wmarnich@summa.es

GARDNER DESIGN
3204 E. Douglas Avenue
Wichita, Kansas 67208
Tel: 316-691-8808
Fax: 316-691-8818
E-mail: info@gardnerdesign.net

GEE + CHANG DESIGN
38 Bryant Street, Suite 100
San Francisco, California 94105
Tel: 415-543-1192
Fax: 415-543-6088
E-mail: earl@geechungdesign.com

GIORGIO DAVANZO DESIGN
32 Belmont Avenue E #506
Seattle, Washington 98102-6306
Tel: 206-328-5031
Fax: 206-324-3592
E-mail: info@davanzodesign.com

GIORGIO ROCCO COMMUNICATIONS
Via Domenichino 27
Milano 20149 Italy
Tel: 02461723/02461726
Fax: 02461728
E-mail: grcom@iol.it

GIOVANNI DESIGN ASSOCIATES
230 E. 44th Street
New York, New York 10017
Tel: 212-972-2145
E-mail: GDA70@earthlink.net

GOTHBERG + CO. DESIGN
Skarsgatan 66, Se-Y1269
Göteberg, Sweden
E-mail: design@gothberg.se

GRAIF DESIGN
165 E. Highway CC
Nixa, Missouri 65714
Tel: 417-725-1091
Fax: 417-725-6254
E-mail: matt@7coursedesign.com

GRANT DESIGN COLLABORATIVE
111 E. Marietta Street
Canton, Georgia 30114
Tel: 770-479-8280
Fax: 770-479-4384
E-mail: bill@grantcollaborative.com

GREGORY THOMAS ASSOCIATES
2812 Santa Monica Blvd., #201
Santa Monica, California 90404
Tel: 310-315-2192
Fax: 310-315-2194
E-mail: gregory@gtabrands.com

GRETEMAN GROUP
1425 E. Douglas, Suite 200
Wichita, Kansas 67211
Tel: 316-263-1004
Fax: 316-273-1060
E-mail: sgreteman@gretemangroup.com

GRIFFIN DESIGN
RR22, Box 6
1426 Butchers Lane
Blooming, Illinois 61701
Tel: 309-829-4295
E-mail: tracy@griffindesign.net

HAND MADE GROUP S. R. L.
via Sartori, 16
52017 Stia (Ar)
Italy
Tel: 39 0575 582083
Fax: 39 0575 582198
E-mail: handmade@dada.it

HOFFMAN ANGELIC DESIGN
317-1675 Martin Drive
Surrey, British Columbia V4A 6E2
Canada
Tel: 604-535-8551
Fax: 604-535-8551
E-mail: hoffman_angelic@telus.net

HOHENHORST ADVERTISING AGENCY
Never Kamp 30
Hamburg 20357 Germany
Tel: 49 171 1772127
Fax: 49 40 43209163
E-mail: etthing@foumat-UU.com

HORNALL ANDERSON DESIGN WORKS, INC.
1008 Western Avenue, Suite 600
Seattle, Washington 98104
Tel: 206-467-5800
Fax: 206-467-6411
E-mail: info@hadw.com

HUDDLESTON MALONE DESIGN
56 Exchange Place
Salt Lake City, Utah 84111
Tel: 801-595-6080
Fax: 801-595-6841
E-mail: dmalone@hmd.com

IE DESIGN
1600 Rosecrans Avenue
Building 6B
Manhattan Beach, California 90266
Tel: 310-727-3500
E-mail: mail@iedesign.net

INOX DESIGN
Via Terraggio II
Milan, Italy
Tel: 0039 02 8057007
Fax: 0039 02 8056283
E-mail: info@inoxdesign.it

INTRAWARE, INC.
2000 Powell Street
Emeryville, California 94333
Tel: 925-253-6523
Fax: 510-597-4851
E-mail: r-di@intraware.com

IT IS DESIGN CO.
204 Patio Harajuku, 3-15-22
Jingumae, Tokyo 150-0001
Japan
Tel: 03 3408 5753
Fax: 03 3408 7773
E-mail: itis@so-net.ne.jp

JILL TANNENBAUM GRAPHIC DESIGN & ADV.
4701 Sangamore Road, Suite 2355
Bethesda, Maryland 20816
Tel: 301-229-1135
Fax: 301-320-6620
E-mail: jill@jtdesign.com

JOSE J. DIAS DA S. JUNIOR
R. Nilza Medeiros Martins 275/103
05628-010 Sao Paulo, Brazil
Tel: 5511 37422996
Fax: 5511 8813887
E-mail: jjjunior1@ig.com.br

JULIA TAM DESIGN
2216 Via La Brea
Palos Verdes, California 90274
Tel: 310-378-7583
Fax: 310-378-4589
E-mail: taandm888@earthlink.net

KESSELKRAMER
Lauriergracht 39
Amsterdam 1016 RG
Netherlands
Tel: 31 20 530 1060
Fax: 31 20 530 7067
E-mail: special-k@kesselskrammer.nl

KAN & LAU DESIGN CONSULTANTS
28/F Great Smart Tower
230 Wanchai Road
Hong Kong
Tel: 852 2574 8399
Fax: 852 2572 0199
E-mail: design@kanandlau.com

LA WEEKLY
6715 Sunset Boulevard
Los Angeles, California 90028
Tel: 323-993-3561
E-mail: bsmith@laweekly.com
E-mail: sscott@laweekly.com
E-mail: dcollins@laweekly.com

LEE REEDY CREATIVE
1542 Williams Street
Denver, Colorado 80218
Tel: 303-333-2936
Fax: 303-333-3046
E-mail: lreedy@leereedy.com

LIBBY PERSZYK KATHMAN
19 Garfield Place
Cincinnati, Ohio 45202
Tel: 513-241-6401
Fax: 513-241-0417
E-mail: krisha_folden@lpkdesign.com

LORENZ ADVERTISING
9320 Chesapeake Drive, #214
San Diego, California 92123
Tel: 858-268-0291
Fax: 858-268-1146
E-mail: arne@lorenzadvertising.com

LOUEY/RUBINO DESIGN GROUP INC.
2525 Main Street, Suite 204
Santa Monica, California 90405
Tel: 310-396-7724
Fax: 310-396-1686
E-mail: studio@loueyrubino.com

LOWERCASE, INC.
213 W. Institute Place, Suite 311
Chicago, Illinois 60610
Tel: 313-274-0652
Fax: 312-274-0659
E-mail: sdvorak@lowercaseinc.com

MAGMA
Bachstraße 43
76185 Karlsruhe
Germany
Tel: 49 721 929 1970
Fax: 49 721 929 1980
E-mail: magma@magma-ka.com

MCMONIGLE & ASSOCIATES
818 E. Foothill Blvd.
Monrovia, California 91016
Tel: 626-303-1090
Fax: 626-303-5431
E-mail: david@mcmonigle.com

MELISSA PASSEHL DESIGN
1275 Lincoln Avenue, Suite 7
San Jose, California 95125
Tel: 408-294-4422
Fax: 408-294-4104
E-mail: ideasmpd@ihot.com

MICHAEL COURTNEY DESIGN
121 East Boston
Seattle, Washington 98102
Tel: 206-329-8188
Fax: 206-325-8256
E-mail: karen@michaelcourtneydesign.com

MICHAEL PATRICK PARTNERS
532 Emerson Street
Palo Alto, California 94301
Tel: 650-327-3185
Fax: 650-327-3189
E-mail: connie@mppinc.com

MORLA DESIGN
463 Bryant Street
San Francisco, California 94107
Tel: 415-543-6548
Fax: 415-543-7214
E-mail: dan@morladesign.com

O & J DESIGN
10 West 19th Street, 6th Floor
New York, New York 10011
Tel: 212-242-1080
Fax: 212-242-1081
E-mail: box1@designcarrot.com

ODEN MARKETING AND DESIGN
22 N. Front Street, Suite 300
Memphis, Tennessee 38103
Tel: 901-578-8055
Fax: 901-578-1911
E-mail: ssimmons@oden.com

OH BOY, A DESIGN COMPANY
49 Geary Street, Suite 530
San Francisco, California 94108
Tel: 415-834-9063
Fax: 415-834-9396
E-mail dbound@ohboyco.com

141 SINGAPORE PTE LTD
100 Beach Road #32-10 Beach Road
Singapore 189702
Tel: 65 392 9141
Fax: 65 392 9208
E-mail: onefouronespg@onefourone.com.sg

PALMQUIST CREATIVE
P. O. Box 325
Bozeman, Montana 59771
Tel: 406-587-2244
E-mail: Kurt@palmquistcreative.com

PARSONS PROMOTION DESIGN
66 Fifth Avenue
New York, New York 10001
Tel: 212-229-8905
Fax: 212-229-5113
E-mail: kime@newschool.edu

PENSARE DESIGN GROUP, LTD
729 15th Street, NW, 2nd Floor
Washington, DC 20005
Tel: 202-638-7700
Fax: 202-347-8430
E-mail: pensare@saggio.com

PEPE GIMENO-PROYECTO GRAFICO
C/Cadiers, s.n. Pol. d'Oradors
Godella, Valencia E-46110
Spain
Tel: 34 96 390 40 74
Fax: 34 96 390 49 76
E-mail: gimeno@ctv.es

PETERSON & CO.
2200 N. Lamar, Suite 310
Dallas, Texas 75202
Tel: 214-954-0522
Fax: 214-954-1161
E-mail: kristi@peterson.com

PISARKIEWICZ MAZUR & CO INC.
1 Wall Street Court
New York, New York 10005
Tel: 212-668-8400
Fax: 212-668-1366
E-mail: info@designpm.com

R2 DESIGN
Prçt D
Nuno Àlvares Periera, 20 5º FQ
Matosinhos 4450-218
Portugal
Tel: 351 229 386 865
Fax: 351 229 389 482
E-mail: r2design@mail.telepac.pt

R & M ASSOCIATE GRAFICI
Castellammare Distabia
Italia
Tel: 081-8705053
Fax: 081-8728505
E-mail: info@rmassociati.com

RBMM
7007 Twin Hills, #200
Dallas, Texas 75231
Tel: 214-987-6529
Fax: 214-987-3662

REVOLUZION STUDIO FÜR DESIGN
Uhlandstrasse 4
Neuhausen ob Eck 78579
Germany
Tel: 0049 7467 1467
Fax: 0049 7467 91155
E-mail: info@revoLUZion.com

SACKETT DESIGN ASSOCIATES
2103 Scott Street
San Francisco, California 94115
Tel: 415-929-4800
Fax: 415-929-4819
E-mail: elisalindenmeyer@sackettdesign.com

SAGMEISTER INC.
222 West 14th Street
New York, New York 10011
Tel: 212-647-1789
Fax: 313-647-1788
E-mail: ssagmeiste@aol.com

SAMATAMASON
101 South First Street
Des Plaines, Illinois 60016
Tel: 847-428-8600
Fax: 847-428-6564
E-mail: susan@samatamason.com

SAYLES GRAPHIC DESIGN
3701 Beaver Avenue
Des Moines, Iowa 50310
Tel: 515-279-2922
Fax: 515-279-0212
E-mail: sayles@salyesdesign.com

SHAMLIAN ADVERTISING
10 E. Sprout Road
Springfield, Pennsylvania 19064
Tel: 610-338-0570
Fax: 610-338-0675
E-mail: bigopen@aol.com

SHIBLEY PETEET DESIGN
3232 McKinney Avenue, Suite 1200
Dallas, Texas 75202
Tel: 214-969-1050
Fax: 214-969-7585
E-mail: candle@spddallas.com

SOMMESE DESIGN
481 Glenn Road
State College, Pennsylvania 16803
Tel: 814-238-7484
Fax: 814-865-1158
E-mail: lxs14@psu.edu

STOLTZE DESIGN
49 Melcher Street
Boston, Massachusetts 02210
Tel: 617-350-7109
Fax: 617-482-1171
E-mail: john@stoltzedesign.com

SPATCHURST DESIGN ASSOCIATES
230 Crown Street
Darlinghurst, Sydney NSW 2010
Australia
Tel: 61 2 9360 6755
Fax: 61 2 9380 5974
E-mail: steven@spatchurst.com.au

SUMMA COMUNICACIO
Roger de Lluria 124
Barcelona 08037 Spain
Tel: 34 93 459 1477
Fax: 34 93 459 1816
E-mail: wmarnich@summa.es

TRACY DESIGN COMMUNICATIONS INC.
118 S.W. Boulevard
Kansas City, Missouri 64108
Tel: 816-421-0606
Fax: 816-421-0177
E-mail: jantracy@swbell.net

TRICKETT & WEBB LTD.
The Factory
84 Marchmont Street
London WCIN IAG England
United Kingdom
Tel: 020 7388 5832
Fax: 020 7387 4287

TYCOON GRAPHICS
402 Villa Gloria
2-13-7 Jingumae, Shibuya-ku
Tokyo 150-0001 Japan
Tel: 81 3 5411 5341
Fax: 81 3 5411 5342
E-mail: mail@tyg.co.jp

UNIVERSITY OF IOWA FOUNDATION
One West Park Road
Iowa City, Iowa 52244-4550
Tel: 319-335-3305
Fax: 319-335-3310
E-mail: teresa-black@uiowa.edu

WAGNER DESIGN
1018 Fuller Street
Ann Arbor, Michigan 48104
Tel: 734-998-7120

WITHERSPOON ADVERTISING
1000 West Weatherford
Fort Worth, Texas 76102
Tel: 817-339-1373
E-mail: acomtois@witherspoon.com

ZAPPATA DISENADORES S.C.
Lafayete 143 Apzunes 11590
Mexico City, Mexico
Tel: 52 03 4075
Fax: 52 03 5667
E-mail: zappata@prodigy.net.mx

INDEX

Advertising International Limited 157

After Hours Creative 33, 112

Alternatives 66

Arias Associates 69, 113, 114

The Art Institute of Seattle 145

ARTiculation Group/Wilco Design 170

Aspen Interactive 116

Austin Design 93

AXIS Communications 118, 198

Base Art Co. 11

BBK Studio 85

Bloch + Coulter Design Group 42

Bolt 186

The Bonsey Design Partnership 39

Burrows 82

Carbone Smolan Agency 102

Clarity Coverdale Fury 88

Country Companies Design Services 24

Cox Design 36

Creative Conspiracy, Inc. 68

Critt Graham + Associates 14, 16

Cross Colours Ink 44

Damion Hickman Design 63

Dana Collins 194

Danette Angerer 155

David Lemley Design 98, 99, 100

DBD International, Ltd. 132, 135

Didier Saco Design 139

Dinnick & Howells 67

Douglas Joseph Partners 54

Edelman Public Relations Worldwide, ENKI 46

Emery Vincent Design 13, 56, 59, 160

Erbe Design 123, 154

Fitch 86, 171, 176, 178

Foco Media gmbh & cte 173

Fork Unstable Media GMBH 165

Fossil 40, 74

Future Brand, London 187

Gardner Design 76, 154

Gee + Chung Design 38, 105, 142

Giorgio Davanzo Design 58

Giorgio Rocco Communications 70

Giovanni Design Associates 139

Göthberg + Co. Design 153

Graif Design 164

Grant Design Collaborative 27, 81

Gregory Thomas Associates 10

Greteman Group 47, 75, 190

Griffin Design 146

Hand Made Group 26, 37, 71

Hoffman Angelic Design 185

Hohenhorst Advertising Agency 75

Hornall Anderson Design Works, Inc. 35, 130

Huddleston Malone Design 96

IE Design 109, 169, 195

Inox Design 101, 194, 200

Intraware, Inc. 48

IT IS DESIGN Co. 184

Jill Tannenbaum Graphic Design & Adv. 97

José J. Dias da S. Junior 57

Julia Tam Design 92

Kesselskramer 18, 60, 94

Kan & Lau Design Consultants 70, 167

LA Weekly 20, 201

Lee Reedy Creative 80, 131

Libby Perszyk Kathman 168

Lorenz Advertising 49, 79

Louey/Rubino Design Group Inc. 180

Lowercase, Inc. 199

Magma 163

McMonigle & Associates 117

Melissa Passehl Design 22

Michael Courtney Design 31

Michael Patrick Partners 28, 30

Morla Design 83

O & J Design 140

Oden Marketing and Design 72, 110, 111

Oh Boy, A Design Company 141, 147, 174, 197

141 Singaport Pte Ltd 53, 65

Palmquist Creative 66

Parsons Promotion Design 143

Pensaré Design Group, Ltd 151

Pepe Gimeno — Proyecto Gráfico 78

Peterson & Co 122

Pisarkiewicz Mazur & Co Inc. 106

R2 Design 189

R & M Associate Grafici 64

RBMM 125

RevoLUZion—Studio für Design 12

Sackett Design Associates 77

Sagmeister Inc. 89

SamataMason 41, 45, 150

Sayles Graphic Design 73, 119, 192

Shamlian Advertising 142

Sibley Peteet Design 67, 120

Sommese Design 193

Stoltze Design 126

Spatchurst Design Associates 196

Summa Comunicació 128

Tracy Design Communications Inc. 107, 108

Trickett & Webb Ltd. 191

Tycoon 87

University of Iowa Foundation 148

Wagner Design 138

Witherspoon Advertising 121, 175

Zappata Diseñadores S.C. 61, 62, 140